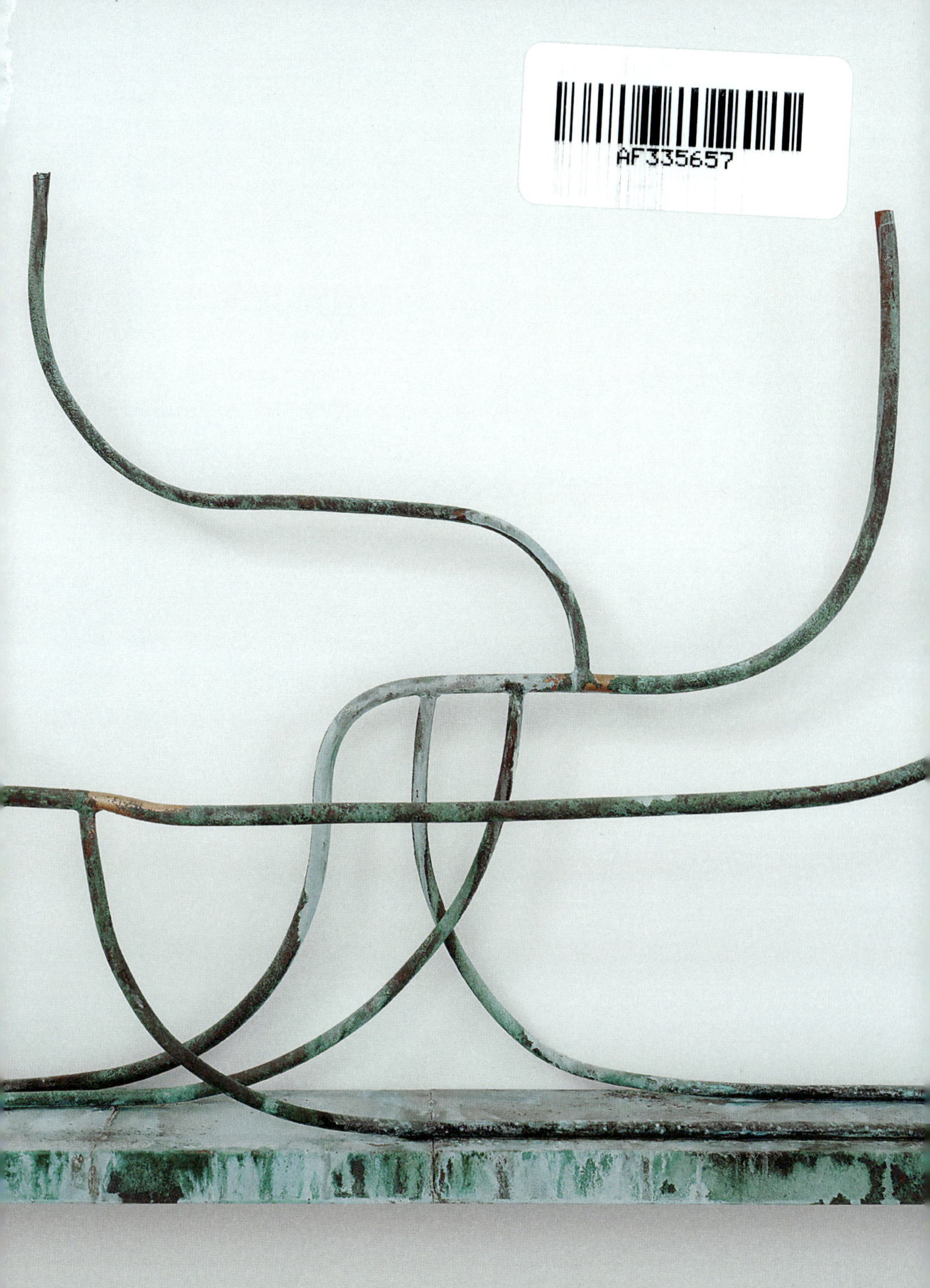
AF335657

WILFRID ALMENDRA
LIGHT BOILED
LIKE LIQUID SOAP

FOGO ISLAND ARTS

Sternberg Press

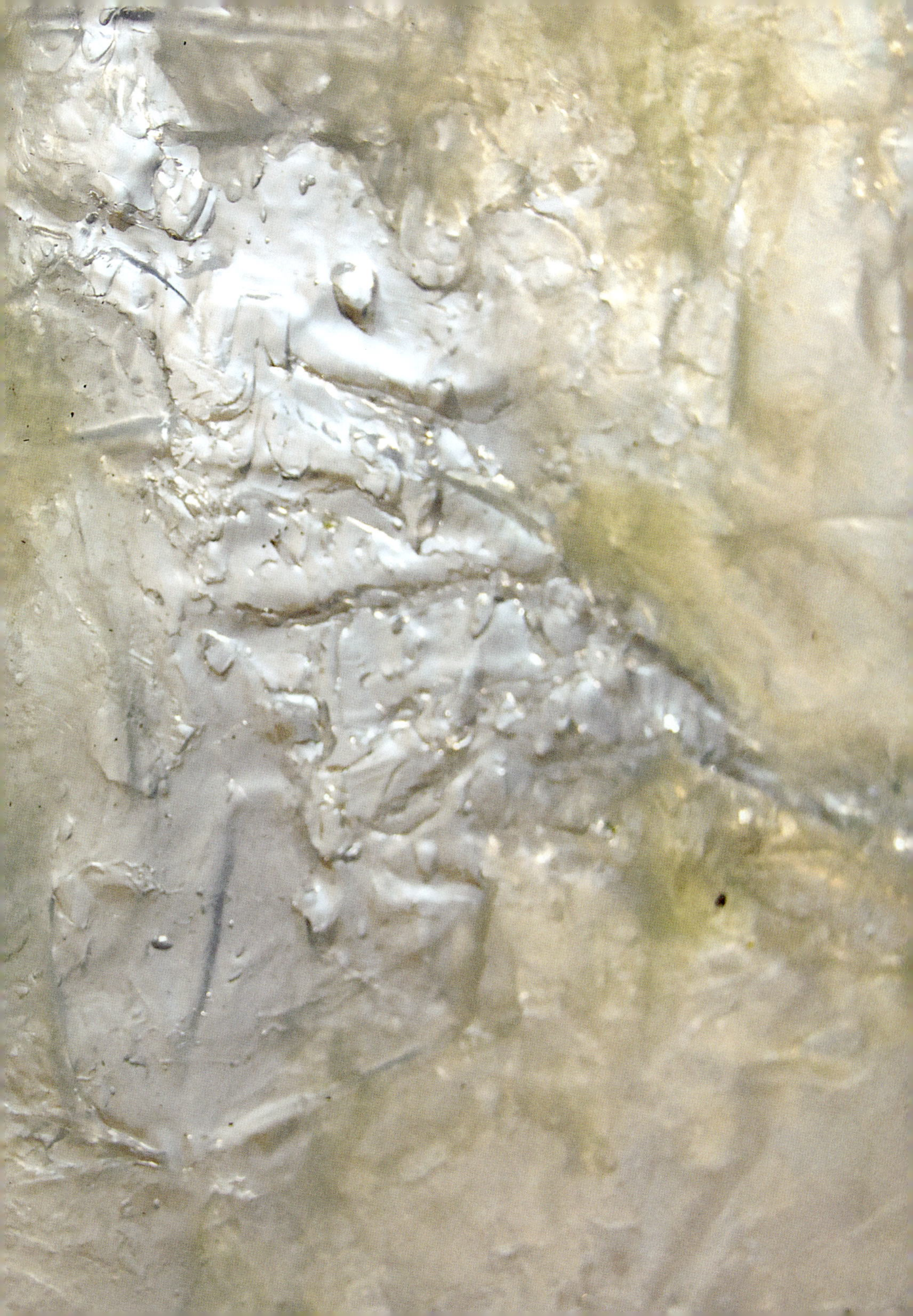

SILICONE VALLEY
NICOLAS IDIER

FRAGMENTS

1

- She watches the light through the translucent curtains. She's calm, happy; she's finally reached the heart of the island. At night she stretches beneath one of the panels that float in the thick air. It's been an eternity since anything but black dust rained from the sky. She retains the memory of rain. Light water that fell to the earth in droplets. That was before.

- Serpents slither in the shadows. They twist over razor-blade-sharp rocks. The two little needles of their teeth spark light. Night after night, she hears the sound of their metallic bodies moving against the ridge of rocks. There are dogs, too.

- She is surprised to feel Bharaiva's warm and humid breath against her earlobes. She's quick. In a single motion, she grabs the knife she keeps at her side and spins around. She faces the threat. Her foot is hurt, it bleeds. She doesn't feel the pain.

- Bharaiva is there. Huge, with shining eyes, fur red as fire. He growls. He frightens her. The blade spurts from her tight fist, ready to attack. Sensing the dog's fear, she slowly lowers the knife. Bharaiva drops down onto his stomach. He places his head onto his two front paws and looks at her. His eyes are white. She understands that the dog is a seer, a guide. His ears shift. She proposes that he stay here with her, in the shelter, to help her. They are there, the two of them, on the middle of the island. They sleep beneath panels from which the large, translucent curtains are suspended. At night, the curtains radiate a boreal light. They shine with the same light as that of her stomach, her breasts, her genitals, which she caresses in silence until her body arcs upward.

- Dark blue, greenish, almost black veins etch along her stomach. Her skin is very white. As white and transparent as the salt rocks Bharaiva licks with his long, sandpaper tongue. The light shines through it. She sleeps naked.

Her nakedness renders her invisible. The shadows can't get her. They can't see her. Only the serpents with their electric sensitivity must be feared.

• The first day, a single, very fine vein travelled her body crosswise. Then a second vein, then more, still finer, appeared. Her stomach now resembles the delta of a large river. She runs her hand over it, and down towards the sea.

• The plastic undulates, it shivers. She caresses it, reassures it, because, like Bharaiva, it's frightened. She speaks to it in a low voice, in whispered words that can't be heard.

• Days and nights pass. Snakes. Bharaiva crushes them with a swift click of his jaw. She crosses the space behind the translucent curtains. She walks toward the sea. She watches the waves crash against the jetty.

• A bench. Against the little wooden church. There hasn't been anyone on the island for a long time. Their god is inside the church, hung on a pale wooden cross. He's like her. Alone, patient. A stranger to this place. At his feet, a drift of cylindrical wrappers and razor blades spread out along the ground, long copper tubes and a blowpipe tied to a dirty orange bottle of gas. This god's is a strange religion, she tells herself, testing the motion of her lips. She waits, seated on the bench, facing the sea. She knows he'll come.

• There must be a secret in this light. Something must exist behind the light. She looks at the light. The light goes through the skin of her face, it moves through her. She watches it undulate gently, as if the wind could make the light undulate. She feels the light move through her and through the veins that progress along the mottled skin of her stomach.

• She learns to dig inside herself to overcome her mounting fear. Her lungs can only fill halfway. She would like them to open, to fill them with light. He'd said to her, *Within you is a sky vaster and more luminous than the sky itself.* He'd added, *I left you alone to discover it.*

- She brought the copper tubes back. She didn't want to bother with the razor blades, viscous with a vinegary matter. The tubes vibrate, undulate, and she hears a voice behind these vibrations. She listens. It speaks to her. The voice answers her. There is Bharaiva and there is the voice.

2

• End of the day. The sun streams diagonally through the glass bay window. I'm in my exercise room, rowing while watching a classic American film. I receive a call from an artist friend I've known for a long time who also works on the possible evolutions of plastic. He tells me he's going to Fogo. When he says that word, Fogo, I think of the Japanese fish with the little poisoned gland.

> "Fogo, with an 'o,' you're confusing it with the *fugu*."
> "Where is it?"
> "In the Gulf of Saint Lawrence."
> "It's an island?"
> "Yes, an island in the middle of the ocean. I'm going to work there for several weeks. You wouldn't want to write an accompanying text?"
> "Wait, I'll call you back. A monkey just climbed into the garden. I think it's going to attack the children. I'll call you back."

• I didn't call him back. There wasn't any monkey in the garden, and I don't have any children. Wilfrid knows that. I live on the thirty-third floor with a view to the clouds, in an enormous apartment blanketed in soft, white carpeting. I never invite anyone over and the carpet is immaculate. After the phone call, I lie down on the carpet, move my head slowly. I wonder if this carpet with its dazzling whiteness doesn't contribute a little to my misanthropy. I start the music with a voice command. Chopin recorded by Martha Argerich. Piano Sonata No. 3 in B minor, Opus 58 floods the apartment, travels through the open window to Shenzhen.

• My laboratory is working on developing an enzyme capable of digesting plastic. The group that finances my research wants to discover a solution for the accumulation of garbage associated with fossil fuels. This enzyme nourishes itself on garbage and is able to fully assimilate it. The enzyme already exists. My Japanese colleagues have created and isolated it. The problem is that the more it eats, the more it grows, and now the risk is that the enzymes will become a threat even greater than the garbage itself. Their voracity is limitless. It seems that, deprived of plastic or other garbage including radioactive waste, the enzymes attack other matter. The Japanese laboratory did not stipulate if human flesh was part of its possible nutrition but I verified that myself, giving an enzyme a discreetly smuggled sea cucumber after lunch at Luohu's Shangri-La. After having tasted this ultra-high protein food the enzyme refused all other matter. It changed in one fell swoop, from holding a status of saviour to predator. I hit the incineration button and a beam of over three thousand degrees Celcius destroyed it before anyone other than myself could observe its evolution. I didn't have any desire to see my studies suspended by the regulating ethics committee because of some damned principle of precaution.

• The laboratory is in the basement of the building. A special elevator connects it directly to my apartment. My world measures one thousand square metres on the ground and one hundred metres in altitude. The company grants me access to the entire facility, including the pool on the top floor which is suspended between my building and its twin. The pool's floor is clear. I swim over empty space. Fluorescent green grass, closed to the public, stretches below me. I swim to Martha Argerich in my waterproof earphones and sometimes also to Webern Variations Opus 27 played by Glenn Gould. The laboratory also provides me with drugs and alcohol. I could ask for anything and I think I'd get it. My needs are reduced. A few books, some Haut-Médoc, and amphetamines.

• My artist friend doesn't know what I'm doing at the moment. My contract stipulates complete secrecy, without exception. Celibacy was part of the confidentiality clause. It worked out well. I was in the middle of a divorce. My ex-wife, with whom I'd had no children, was undoubtedly grateful to see me go, with an extra bonus of a cheque with six zeroes. A fictional address in New Delhi had been attributed to my name, where I would supposedly work on the development of solar energy in Rajasthan under the umbrella of the same industrial group. Solar energy offered the perfect cover to finance my research.

• In the laboratory, I've erected large silicone panels onto copper armatures. Copper is a highly conductive material. Ideal for electrical tests. The armatures are deep and allow me to inject the enzyme into the material without frightening it. I have noted, in fact, that the matter reacts most violently in these experiments, as if menace provoked it to life.

• Threat enlivens. It's the wind that blows over embers.

3

• A dream. I'm in a car, and the car is attacked by some
  kind of thick, viscous liquid; a little like semen. A whitish,
  living matter, loaded with active tenacity, with an object-
  ive to attain. The matter rises—it's a flash flood. It rises
  along the car doors; it obscures the windows, the dash-
  board, the whole thing, in its humid, soapy dish detergent.
  The car disappears beneath a stringy layer of polymer
  hummus. Imprisoned within the car, I observe with grow-
  ing horror as the glass fractures. Filaments of the matter
  run through to the other side of the glass, progress
  towards my hands, paralyzed on the wheel.

• Conversation: "Hello, can you hear me?"
                         "Yes, did you change your mind?"
                         "I'm not sure. What are you planning
                         to do on your island?"
                         "I'm going to create a revolutionary
                         work. Or a piece of work that will be
                         a revolution."
                         "The piece we've talked about? Do
                         you know the risks you're running?"
                         "We have to try. You know as well as I
                         do that we have to try."
                         "I accept on the condition that I can
                         observe your work process. I need a
                         field study. It isn't impossible that
                         the matter would conduct itself dif-
                         ferently outside the laboratory. Will
                         you be able to install an array of
                         cameras and motion detectors in
                         your studio?"

• The cameras are set up to film two different angles of
  the large room where Wilfrid and his assistant, a young
  man with a very muscular torso who's been with him
  forever, work together. I see them, in their bedraggled
  T-shirts, working from morning to night without any
  sense of etiquette. No doubt they've forgotten I'm here,
  twelve thousand kilometres away, connected to them
  by fibre optics. They use a kind of crane to mount their
  enormous panels. The other camera is placed outside

the building, by a luxury hotel with artist studios, sheltered from rain, snow, and from the salty wind. The cameras film without interruption both night and day. I receive the images but can transmit nothing in return. I take note of the facts, of Wilfrid's gestures; thanks to the motion detectors related to a low-frequency emitter, I try to decode the matter's reactions. Wilfrid and his assistant occasionally engage in combat wrestling; their muscles gleam and pearls of sweat appear on the screen. Their jaws are tight. I watch them detachedly when they rock against a silicone sheet. They're like insects on a spiderweb, like two lab rats coated with a thick gel. I observe them coldly, pupils dilated. I take notes entirely in the nude, sitting at my table designed by Pearl Lam made of Venetian Murano glass before a large bottle of Stoli Elit vodka, distilled from Russian winter wheat and water from a reservoir in the Himalayas, three thousand metres underground, one of the most intact reservoirs on Earth.

• Over just a few days, I observe changes in the plastic's chemical behaviour; a sharp evolution in its reactions. Has it understood that a threat weighs against it? The enzyme, meanwhile, is serene. It is calm as the eye of a storm. As a hunter in a watchtower.

• Observation: The network of materials allows for a kind of communication. Communication or contamination: influence of Element A on Element B of the same nature or of a different but compatible nature.

• Conclusion: It is probable that the silicone is aware of the enzyme's threat of predation.

• Question: How is it possible that an enzyme created in a Japanese laboratory (in Beppu, on the northern part of Kyushu Island) could constitute a threat for a silicone stocked in Canada?

• Hypothesis: Fogo Island was highly regarded by nineteenth-century Japanese cod fishers. Documents conserved on

Fogo were kept in the archives of the National Diet Library, in Tokyo. Would this link between Fogo Island and Japan have been maintained, secretly, grotesquely perhaps? The stakes are considerably high. Access to the Arctic. Immense reserves of oil, fresh water, and fish.

4

- No news from Wilfrid or his assistant for several days. The cameras show an unmoving, static tableau, a frozen image occasionally disturbed by an electric fluctuation that momentarily deforms it. I receive, at several regular intervals, an empty email from an unknown sender. When I answer, the computer displays an error message. I don't understand. At night, my telephone rings but there's no one on the other end. Sometimes I hear, around 10:40 p.m., a loudspeaker broadcasting a hoarse man's voice, but when I look out the window there's nothing but emptiness and city lights. Wilfrid doesn't answer the telephone or his emails. Where is he? I decide to go to Fogo Island. I call the woman in charge of the group with whom I'm in contact to ask her for authorization to travel. She doesn't ask any questions and answers only that everything will be ready the day after tomorrow. "There's time for you to swim a few more laps in the pool," she says dryly.

- Two days later, my bags are packed. A car waits for me in the building's parking lot. I have given precise instructions to my team at the laboratory. The car drives me to Shenzhen station where I take the high-speed train to Hong Kong, and from there, board a plane to Ottawa. Upon my arrival, someone will make arrangements for a helicopter or a boat to Fogo Island. I'm not concerned.

- For a twenty-hour flight between Hong Kong and Ottawa, with a stop in New York, I read the *Tao Te Ching*, the only book I never tire of.

> *One begot two.*
> *Two begot three.*
> *And three begot ten thousand things.*

- I read in Chinese. Between two chapters, I close my eyes. When I open them again, I discover a new passenger. A young woman with very pale eyes and hair so blonde it melts into the snowy light that filters through the porthole.

    "Hello, my name is Hanabi."

• She is seated in the empty seat beside me. First class is usually packed, but today, with the exception of an old, obese Chinese man snoring on the other side of the cabin, Hanabi and I are alone.

> "Your first name is Japanese. Firework."
> "Yes. I prefer fire flower."
> "You don't look Japanese."
> "No? Because of my blonde hair and my blue eyes? But I am Japanese. My father worked on the enzyme. The same one you're working on yourself. I'm up on everything. The *Tao Te Ching*? Good reading. I especially like the axiom 'governing is like frying small fish.'"

• I'm short of breath. How could this person be aware of my research? Moreover, how could she have found me? A panicky sweat glues me to the moulded seat of beige leatherette.

> "Don't worry about it. I'm not a bad person. Your group knows. They've sent me. When they understood you were connected to Wilfrid, your artist friend who went to Fogo Island, they alerted my father immediately. You might be surprised but they finance Wifrid's research, as well as yours. The stakes are far too high to be given to only one laboratory, you understand."

• We arrive in Ottawa. Hanabi has reserved two suites at the Château Laurier, a hotel that resembles a European castle, but bigger. She asks me for my mobile phone. I show a little reticence, but she insists: "We cannot run any risk of being discovered. Starting tonight, we escape the boundaries of surveillance. Give it to me."

• She waits for me at the edge of the pool, reclining on a deck chair. I sit beside her. She wears a white dress through which I can make out the smallest details of her body. She extends a Japanese pack of cigarettes. I take one, and light it with a gold and black lacquer Dupont lighter. My gaze rests on the lighter, which is ornamented with ancient Chinese characters painted in red. Too little to divine their meaning. Other guests linger at the park. The moon is full. Tomorrow, we will be on Fogo Island. I don't know what is waiting for us. Hanabi has not said anything else. When I asked her for news of Wilfrid she was silent. At present, she drinks a Heineken from the bottle, and I've got a gin and tonic. Something about her disturbs me. Not only that she is a spy sent to control me, but something about her body. I look at her again. Anew. It's not, in fact, her dress that's transparent. It's her. Entirely. Hanabi's body shows the light of the moon. Through her, I can see the constellations of the Big and Little Dippers, which I have never seen so up close.

5

• I touched her skin. I wanted to see if I was dreaming. Hanabi leans towards me and kisses me. Her tongue is lively, quick, fresh. Hanabi catches my hand and guides me towards her. She does not seem shy about the presence of the other hotel guests or personnel. The desire I experience is so intense that I come just from touching her. But it's just a sensation, there isn't anything, the sensation is prolonged and is repeated again. We go up to her room. Perhaps she has drugged me. It would explain this sharp floating.

• Stretched along the bed, Hanabi's skin takes on an ever-more-luminous tint. I am making love to a plant operating its photosynthesis. She radiates. I am obliged to close my eyes but I continue, through my eyelids, to see her silhouette of pure light spread out against the carmine silk of the bedcover.

• A plane with propellers, an ATR 42 made of new-generation composite materials, takes us across the Gulf of Saint Lawrence. I watch the flights of wild birds from the plane window. Geese with black wingtips and plump bellies, silver seagulls, puffins with multicoloured beaks. It's a dream of beauty, all these birds. We land in Newfoundland, where we board a fishing boat that takes us to the Fogo Island port. A car is waiting for us. Destination Fogo Island Inn. Where Wilfrid set up, according to his first messages.

• There's not a single element of plastic in this entire immense hotel, constructed on stilts, facing a sea punctuated with large pieces of icebergs that drift in from the Atlantic. The world's heads of state come here to rest behind closed doors and in perfect luxury. The new elite at the time of global warming won't go to Santo Domingo or to other places of unbearable heat but travel rather to Fogo Island and to small Alaskan towns.

• She will swim in waters cooled by the great icicles broken off from the pack ice floe. Artist studios orbit around the Fogo Island Inn like satellites. Wilfrid was supposed to be one of the resident artists. I am surprised to find no one at my arrival. The manager thinks Wilfrid never arrived. He was announced, of course, but had not showed up. The hotel personnel are formal. The studio, set up ten minutes away, in an abandoned church, has remained empty, as has his hotel room. I ask to be taken to the chapel. And yet I recognize the space. I saw it, right here, with my own eyes. Exactly the same as on the videos.

- Hanabi goes to take a sea bath.

> "The water isn't too cold?"
> "It's freezing. I like it."

Why do pretty girls always say things that make you want them? And why am I here, on this island cut off from the world, talking to a nymphomaniac with a transparent face? Hanabi speaks to me of an accident that occurred a few days earlier. A ship vanished at sea, north of Fogo Island. No one knows what it was carrying. I can't help but wonder if there's a link between it and Wilfrid's disappearance.

- The day he arrived, he sent me a notification: "Alone in the world. Magnificent sea. Nighttime storm warnings." The hotel personnel lie. Wilfrid was here, I am convinced that Wilfrid was here. He had his installation project: silicone sheets suspended from a network of copper pipes and wooden slabs. He wanted to work on the network's logic, on its communication, transmission. He wanted to develop a radio stratagem to diffuse the subliminal messages. His project has always attempted to "create a favourable terrain for a new form of life." I knew that he was there, I saw him. I don't understand why they won't tell me the truth.

- My room looks out over the sea. It's the first time I've ever seen icebergs. On the plane, I read an article in the *Journal of Glaciology* about Antarctica's bleeding glaciers, caused by the oxidation of water. The photograph of one of the blood falls fascinated me. An immense cascade of blood pouring out from the dazzling whiteness of a cliff of ice and falling into the scarlet sea. I think of it as I search for sleep, curtains pulled to spare me the movements of the sky, beaten by a strong north wind. Hanabi knocks at my door. She is barefoot.

6

- Between two enormous flat boulders, a copper ladder. It descends below the earth. At about ten metres, metallic cables hold up an enormous wooden platform painted black. Bharaiva has stayed under the stairs. He was lying down to wait. The earth is dry.

- She watches the silicone sheets suspended from the copper pipes beneath the large wooden platforms. Cottony light emanates from them. It smells strongly and she feels as though she's suffocating. She walks slowly into the room. Electrical wires run along the ground, linked to a transmitter with long, curved antenna, a sort of animal, a reindeer, a metallic caribou. Wilfrid extends his hand.

"What is it attached to?"
"To the plastic," answers Wilfrid.
"It's a transmitter-receiver. It uses the copper to send signals. I'm trying to provoke reactions in the plastic. The waves produced by the silicone sheets you see here act on the plastic structure itself."
"For what purpose?"
"To communicate with what is hidden beneath the plastic."
"What's hidden under the plastic?"
"I don't know. There's something there, I'm sure of it, but I don't know what it is. Maybe the plastic protects it, or destroys it. We have to know. We need to figure it out."
"And the silicone, why does it emit signals?"
"It's intelligent silicone. Our capacity to speak to the world is infinite, you know. We learned it millennia ago, to speak to rocks, water, then fire. That was before plastic arrived. Little by little plastic cut us off from the other elements. It covered everything.
It went so far as to cover the man's

genitals in order to prevent fertilizing the woman's womb. With its pretext of security and precaution, the world of humans was entirely transformed into plastic. Until the day where the children themselves will begin to be entrusted to this material. And do you know where we're headed? Towards a world covered in a plastic that has become intelligent, capable of reproducing itself, of moving, of changing shape, anticipating our most basic needs, like food, sex, sleep. Entire parts of the human body have already been colonized by plastic. At first, it was only people who wanted to augment the size of their breasts, or their lips, as well as those survivors of accidents who needed prostheses. Then, scientists, fed by the colossal amounts of money generated by the human race's two greatest desires—physical beauty and longevity—developed, improved, and finally created a new type of plastic. And this plastic, if we do nothing, will toll the bell of the end of a free and independent humanity, surely as well as the dictators have attempted from antiquity until now with their shortsighted ideologies. For there is one point in common in all the enemies of the twentieth century—the visceral need for plastic. No one saw the threat coming and when the plastic had mutated, thanks to the injection of genetic sequences on living tissue, it was already too late."

- He asks her to lie on the ground, beneath one of the great sheets. She closes her eyes. She feels him moving around her, checking the connections, tightening a screw or a bolt or one of the multiple arrangements of the machine. She also feels the sheets of liquid plastic undulate from either side of her prone body.

- The air begins to vibrate. Waves cross the entire planet, skirt the meridians and the magnetic currents of the oceans. The plastic itself is crossed by the magnetic waves. Perhaps someone, out there, in the distance, is trying to send a message; maybe it is a declaration of war, of peace, or of love.

- With the infiltration of plastic into the human body, progressive and inevitable, time was suspended, little by little. No one got old anymore and it became rare to die, except for a violent death. The growth of children stopped. The plastic had finished by colonizing the entire human race, and it was not long before the human genome integrated plastic within its sequence. The process was then complete.

- The silicone sheets are the colour of jade, which reminds her of the sky. Wilfrid holds himself over her. A drop of an unknown, sticky liquid falls against her rounded, pregnant stomach. The drop travels back up to her belly button, fills like a saltwater pool out on the beach, by the sea. She closes her eyes. In the distance, behind the ever-more-opaque silicone panels, shot through with very fine veins, like marble, she hears a voice. A voice that calls to her. She answers with an endless scream.

CONTENTS

PREFACE

ALEXANDRA
MCINTOSH AND
NICOLAUS
SCHAFHAUSEN

First presented at the Fogo Island Gallery in 2016, Wilfrid Almendra's solo exhibition *Light Boiled Like Liquid Soap* is an immersive installation featuring radio transmission and a series of sculptural elements made of copper, plaster, and silicone in various states of dematerialization. Combining found and repurposed materials, the works attest to notions of desire, circulation, and flux, from protective spaces of retreat to global economies of exchange.

The title of the exhibition draws upon Ralph Ellison's *Invisible Man*, as quoted by Fred Moten in his essay "To Feel, to Feel More, to Feel More Than": "The light seemed to boil opalescently, like liquid soap shaken gently in a bottle."[1] Part of a larger reflection on invisibility as a source of agency, the sentence aptly conveys something of the experience of moving through Almendra's installation: a sense of beauty tempered by unease, of the everyday and the rarefied, of porosity and slippages between material properties and mental states. Or, as Almendra describes in conversation with exhibition curators Alexandra McIntosh and Nicolaus Schafhausen, "we're between material and air, solid [and] gel."

Light Boiled Like Liquid Soap transforms the Fogo Island Gallery into an all-encompassing environment. Three floating platforms made of scorched wooden boards, chicken wire, and plaster are suspended from the ceiling. Carbonized black on the upper surface and white underneath, the platforms reference the floor plan of an average house and are hung at standard ceiling height, dividing the vertical space of the gallery in two. Beneath them and at intervals throughout the gallery are large sheets of silicone draped over copper pipes. Translucent and glistening, with amorphous areas of colour and a skin-like texture, the sheets are at once attractive and repellent. The copper pipes thread into and out of the platforms or are curved into freestanding sculptures. A length of PVC pipe wrapped in plaster bandages runs along one wall, branching off and creating an incursion into the space of the gallery.

[1] Ralph Ellison, *Invisible Man*, 2nd ed. (New York: Vintage International, 1995), 345; quoted in Fred Moten, *Black and Blur* (Durham, NC: Duke University Press, 2017), ch. 19.

These formal gestures create spatial relationships that evoke the body and discreetly influence a visitor's movement through the space. Almendra uses commonplace building materials that are, for all their ubiquity, resonant with associations, evoking residential or DIY construction, amateur practices, as well as surgical alteration and healing. Both familiar and destabilizing, the installation takes on the unfinished, transitional qualities of a basement or garage, an environment for experimentation or retreat.

Individually precarious, the works come together as a functioning whole. The copper and silicone sculptures are linked by electrical cables that snake across the floor and act as radio transmitters. Connected to the steel substructure of the gallery, the entire installation and the building itself become a unified, resonant body that diffuses radio waves. The content of the transmission is a series of poems recited in Portuguese that are broadcast every fifteen minutes, pirating the airwaves and conveying their message within a twenty-kilometre radius of the gallery walls. The author, a Portuguese stonemason named Jorge Armando Sousa with whom Almendra collaborated on a previous project, narrates the poems. Clandestine and inaudible in the gallery, the poems nevertheless create points of connection with the external world, picked up in nearby houses or on passing ships, and evoking historic trading routes between Fogo Island and Portugal.

Almendra's approach to making work foregrounds the importance of labour—his own and that of others—as a form of knowledge acquisition that also offers the potential for collaboration and exchange. In many of his projects, the artist has established connections with local makers and artisans out of both necessity and interest. For *Light Boiled Like Liquid Soap*, Almendra incorporated in new form the poems of stonemason Sousa, included in this publication, and collaborated with Fogo Island metalworker Marc Fiset to make the steel brackets that anchor the suspended platforms. More than providing a service, these forms of interaction have the potential to move beyond institutional frameworks and established bodies of knowledge, and privilege informal economies of exchange.

Writing in this volume, Anne Faucheret in "The Promise of the Waves" begins by tracing the lineage of Almendra's practice through the concerns and material explorations of previous works and their evolution within the Fogo Island Gallery installation. *Light Boiled Like Liquid Soap* is found to act as "an ecosystem of interdependent elements, human and non-human, past and present." This interdependence of things is key to understanding Almendra's work and process as a whole. Evoking Caribbean philosopher Édouard Glissant's concepts of archipelagic thinking and creolization, Faucheret grounds Almendra's work as a language of relationships, an emphasis on how parts relate to one another rather than acting as discrete hegemonic entities. With an interest in "the abandoned, the invisible, the inaudible," Almendra's work is seen as embodying a form of nomadism that allows for a rethinking of our relationships to economic and cultural systems of exchange, to time, to ourselves, and to other subjectivities.

Nicolas Idier's "Silicone Valley" is a work of speculative fiction on futuristic and possibly sentient technologies that aim to dispose of plastics but threaten to overwhelm their creators. The short story takes place on an island that may or may not be Fogo and attributes a nefarious ulterior motive to the creation of Almendra's work. The unnamed narrator agrees to become involved in the project on the condition that he be allowed to observe the working process of the artist and his assistant as the exhibition takes shape.

Idier's story emerged from the unique system of communication established between the writer and the artist: a live feed from the gallery space as Almendra and his assistant, Maxime Davy, installed the exhibition. Establishing a link across thousands of kilometres and a nine-hour time difference, the open channel paradoxically seemed to obfuscate rather than enable connection. The story opens a space of desire, eroticism, communication, and contamination between human and nonhuman entities, encapsulating our fears of artificial intelligence and complicity in the destruction of the environment.

In his conversation with McIntosh and Schafhausen, Almendra addresses the installation as a paradoxical space that oscillates between multiple binaries but also conveys his interest in the "indeterminate middle, which is neither one thing nor the other—a zone of encounters and possibilities where categories dissolve [...] it's this precise place of desire and emancipation that [he] wants to locate." Their far-ranging discussion broaches bodily forms of perception in engaging with architectural space, including the work's relationship to the history of modernist architecture and sculpture, acknowledged systems of value production and collaborative practices, and the fragility of communication across territorial boundaries.

Throughout Almendra's work there is a continuity of conceptual concerns and processes, such as his use of everyday materials that are evocative yet unfixed in meaning, as well as his active pursuit of collaboration. Following its presentation on Fogo Island, the project was installed at the Palais de Tokyo, Paris, and enlivened with new radio content from diverse collaborators. These through lines in his work are a form of continuity that align with his material interests and execution. The silicone sheets in the gallery stretch and sag over time, the copper takes on a patina and oxidizes, the plaster gradually turns yellow. It is an exhibition as living organism, where materials are subject to the effects of time and offered autonomy to pursue their innate evolutionary processes. Similarly, Sousa's poems—texts that describe natural spaces gradually reclaimed from human incursions—are an ongoing reflection on the entropic processes of a changing landscape.

Blurring boundaries and foregrounding relationships between things, or in other words, working in the "indeterminate middle," Almendra seems to ask Fred Moten's question: "Can you hold one another tonight in the blur, so that one and another are no more?"[2] With *Light Boiled Like Liquid Soap*, Almendra creates a porousness between entities and subjects, a freedom for natural and chemical processes and the unpredictable results of collaborative practices to occur.

2
Moten, ch. 19.

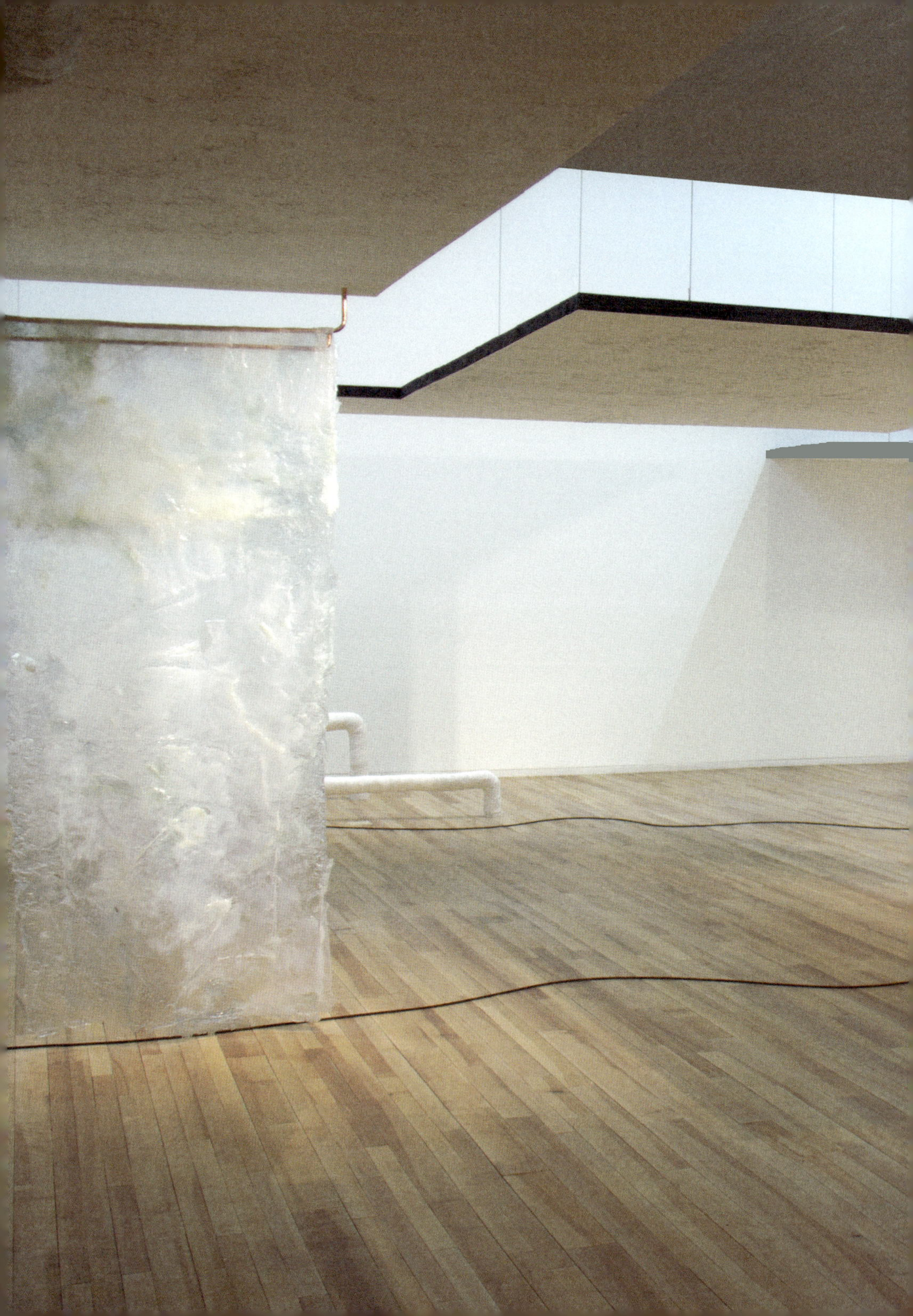

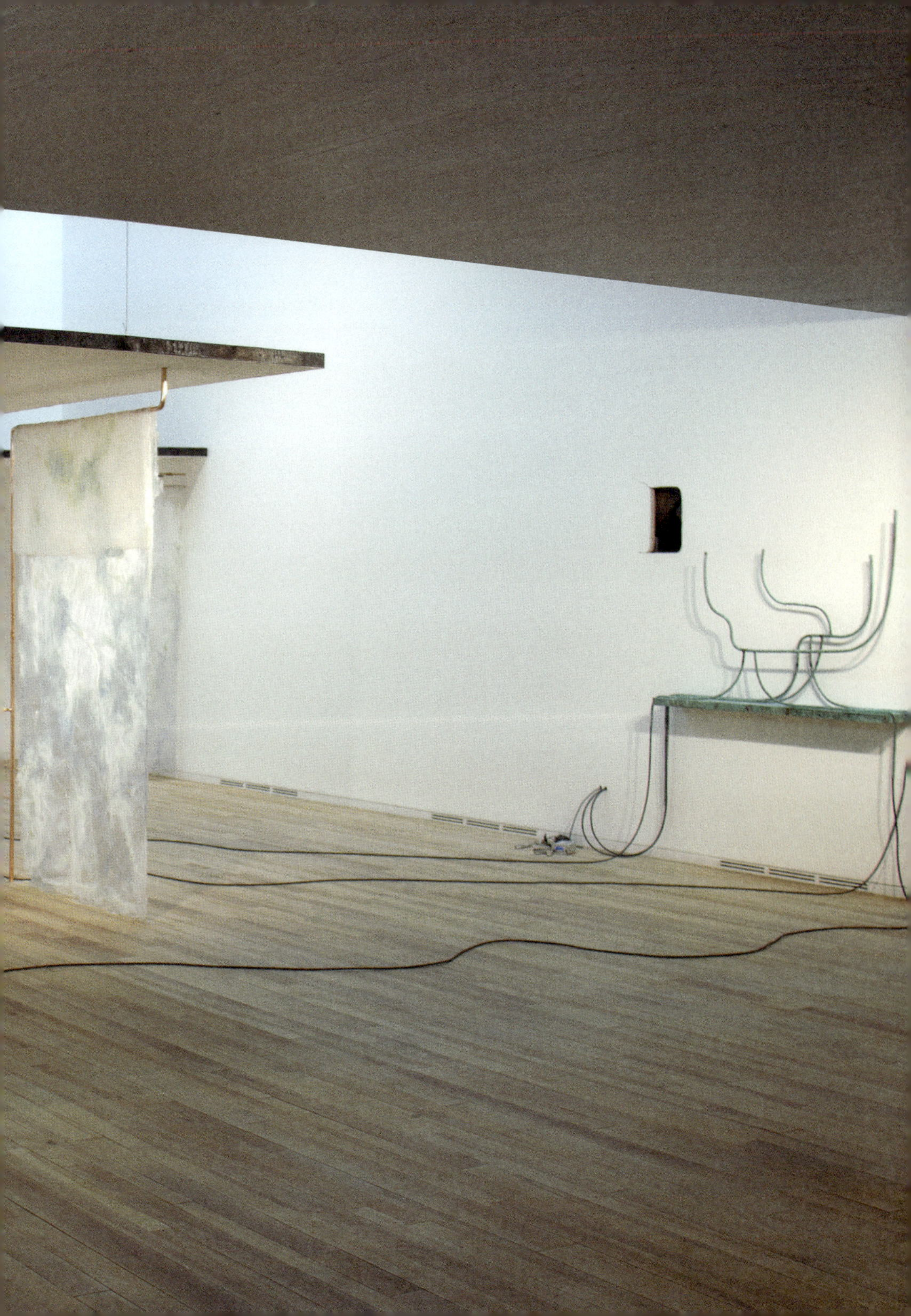

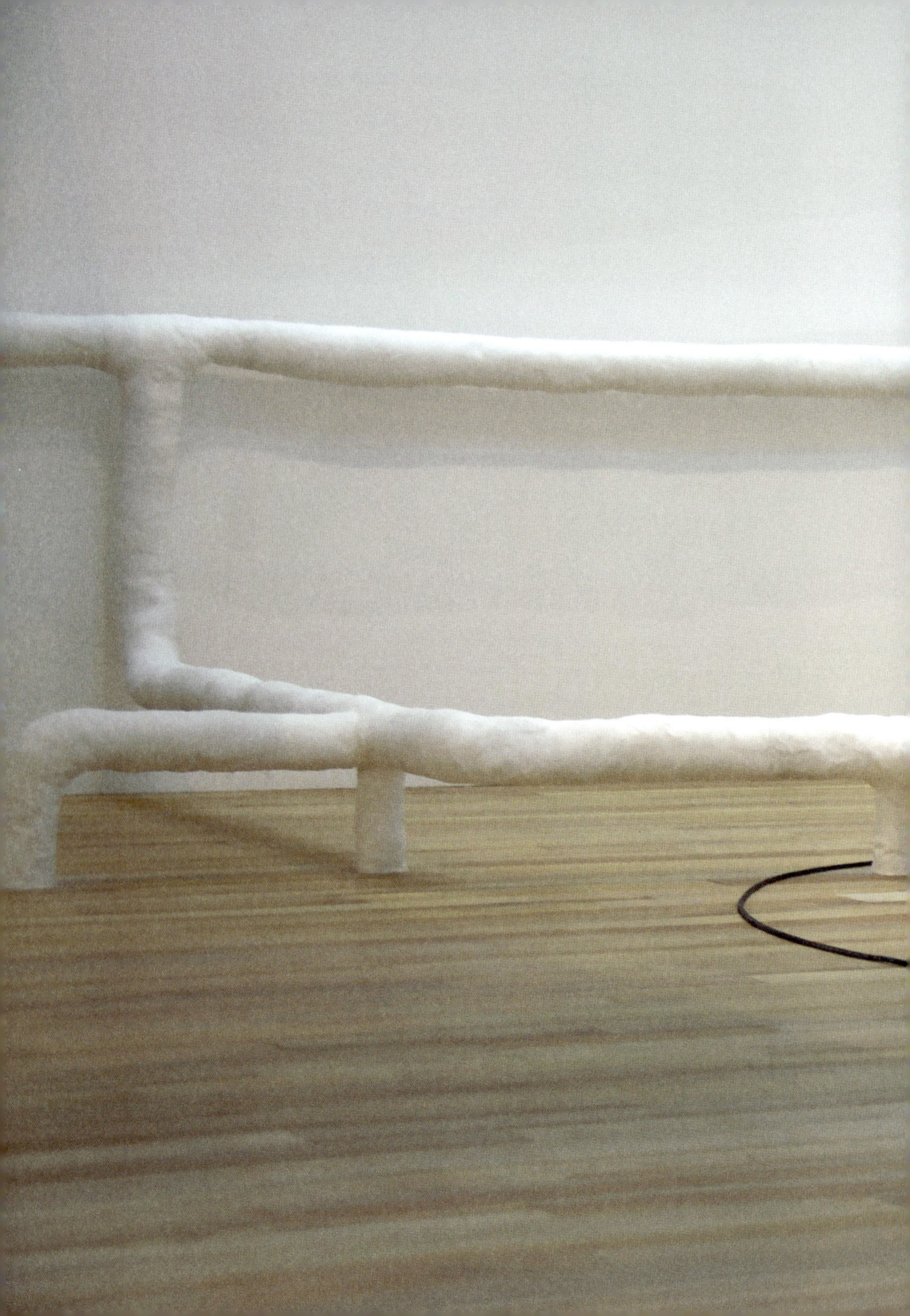

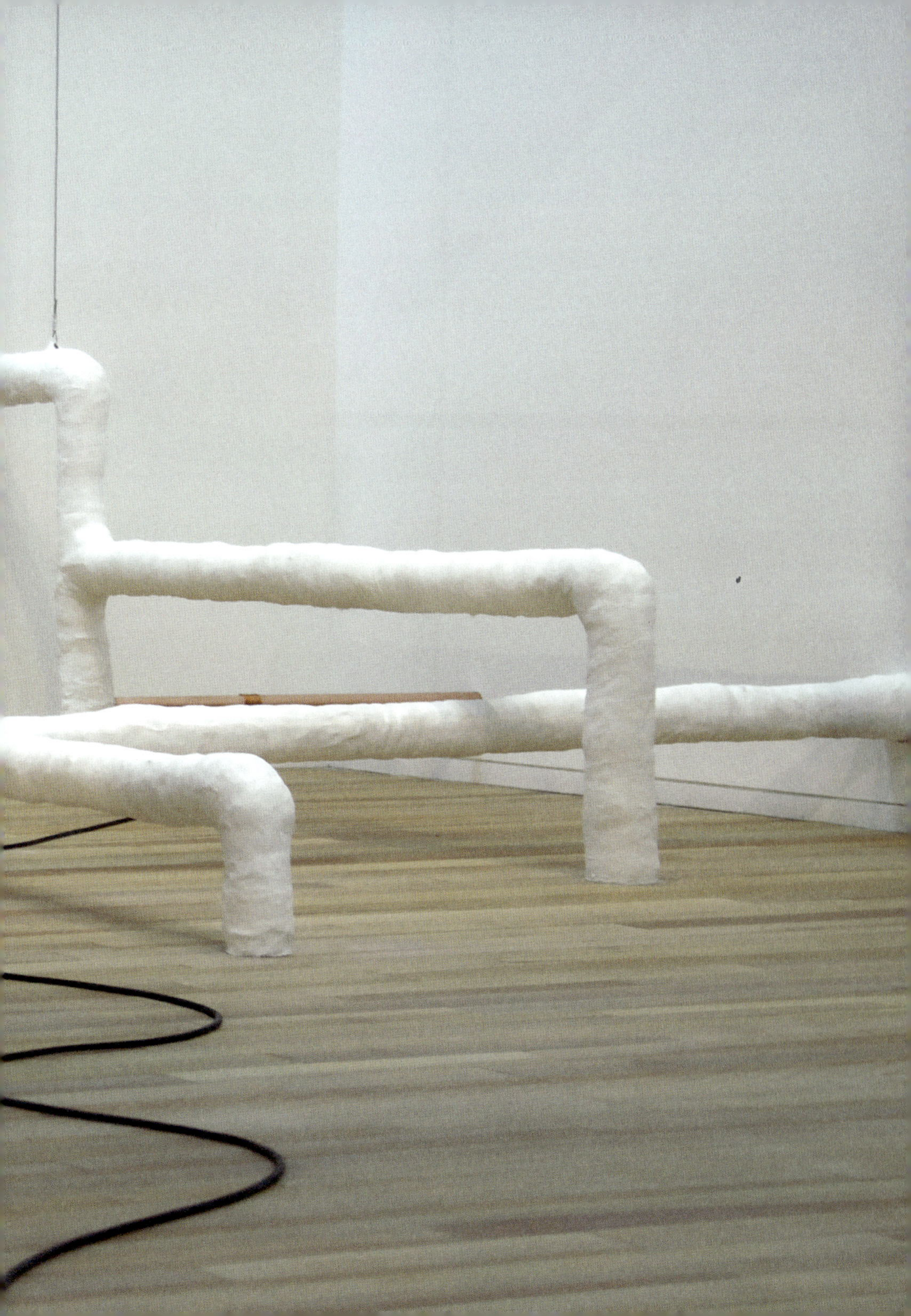

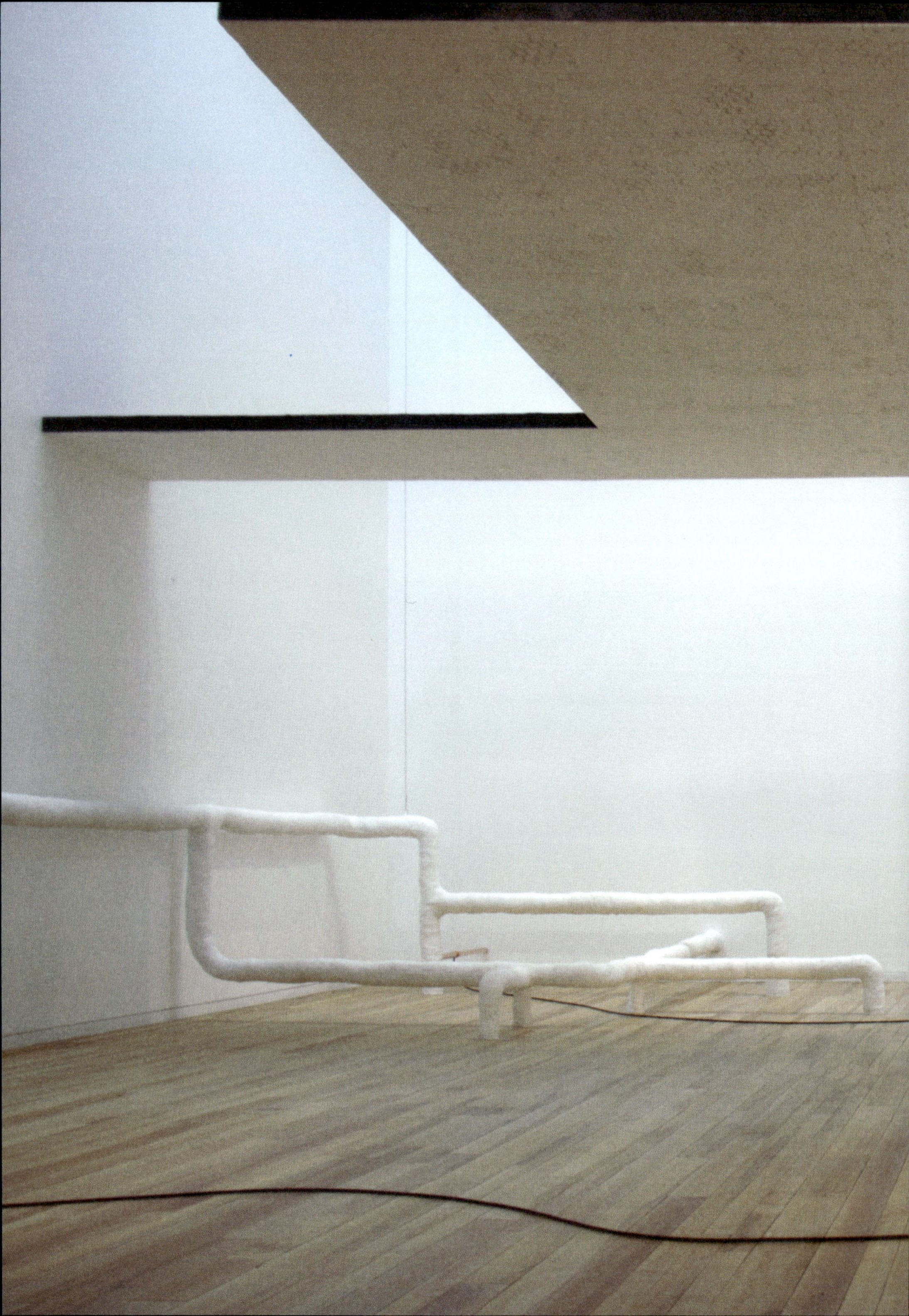

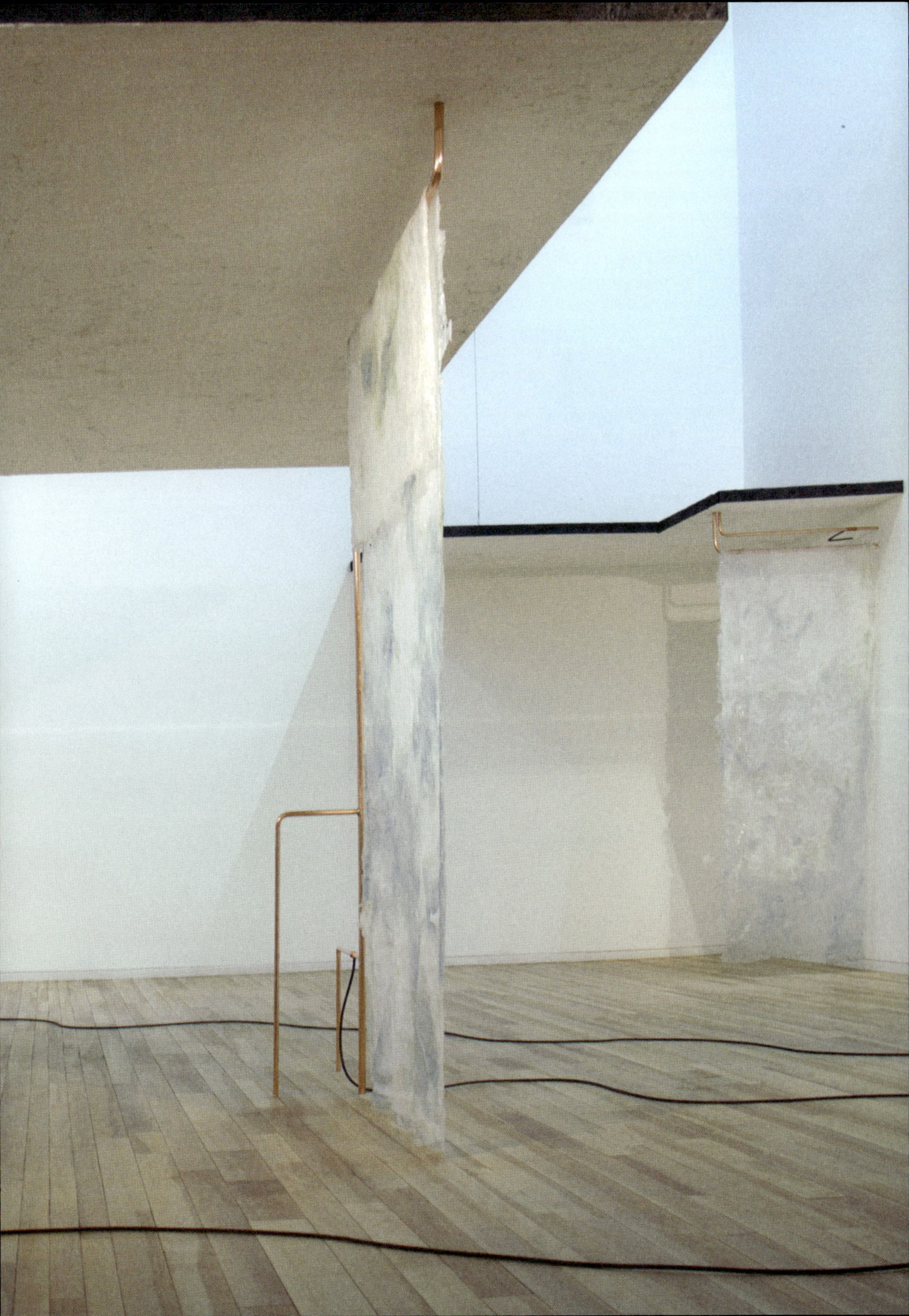

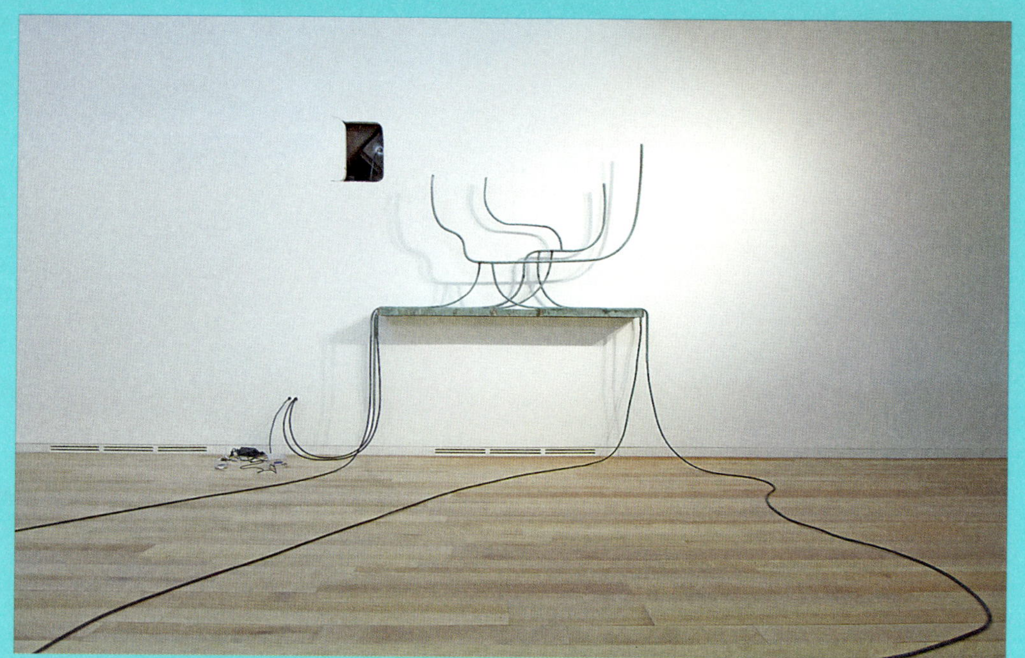

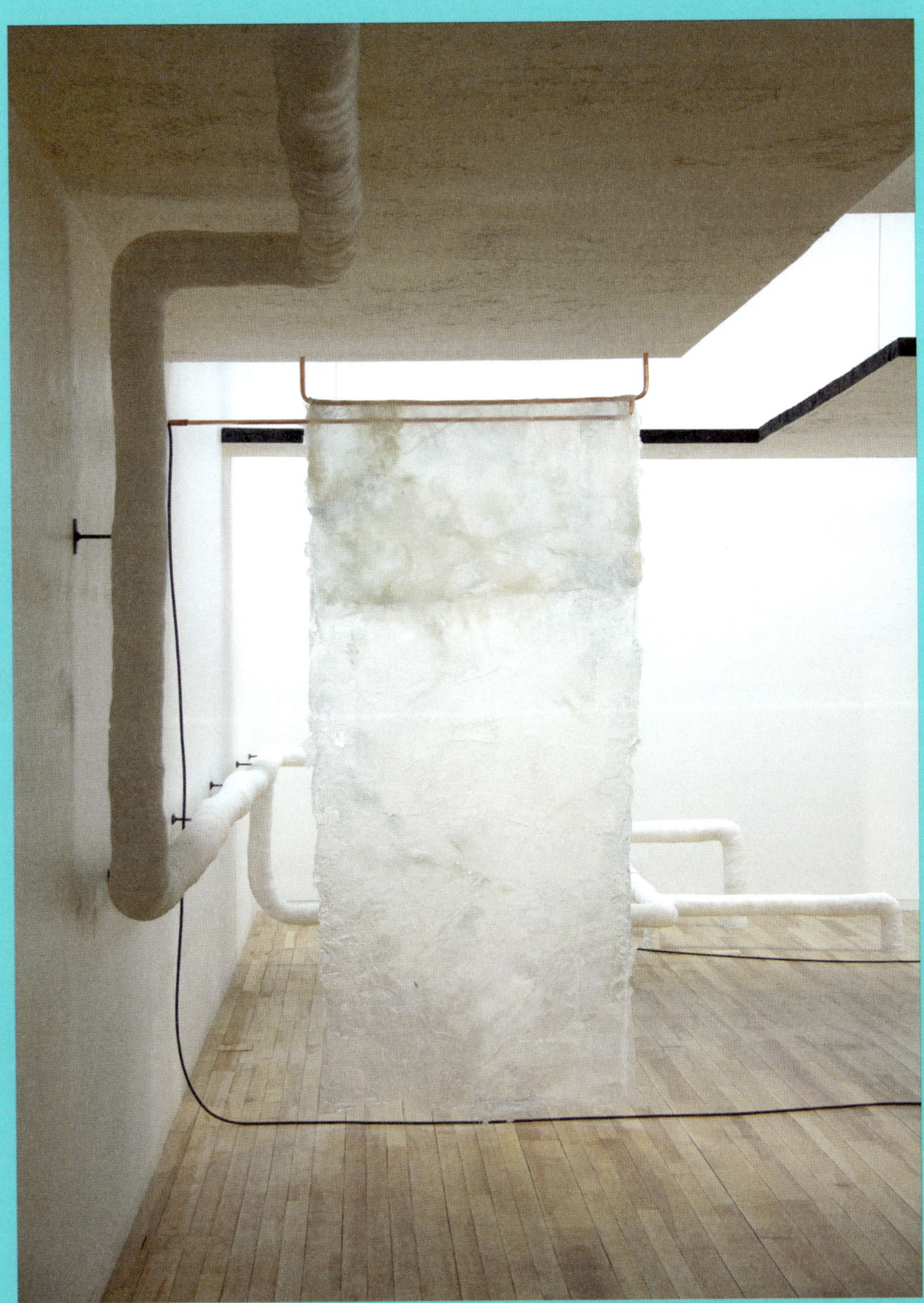

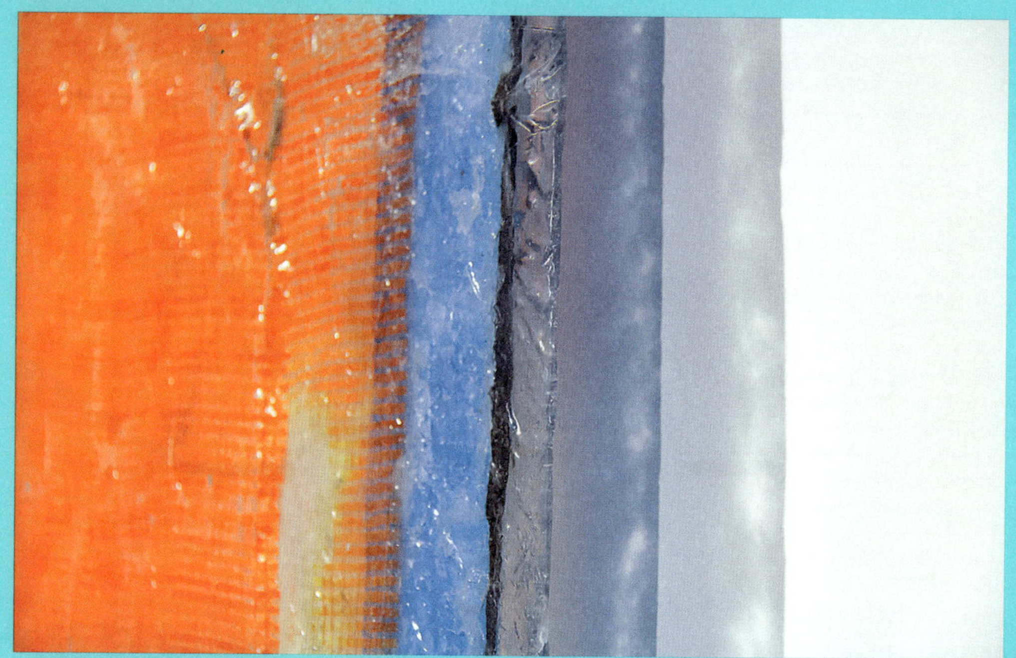

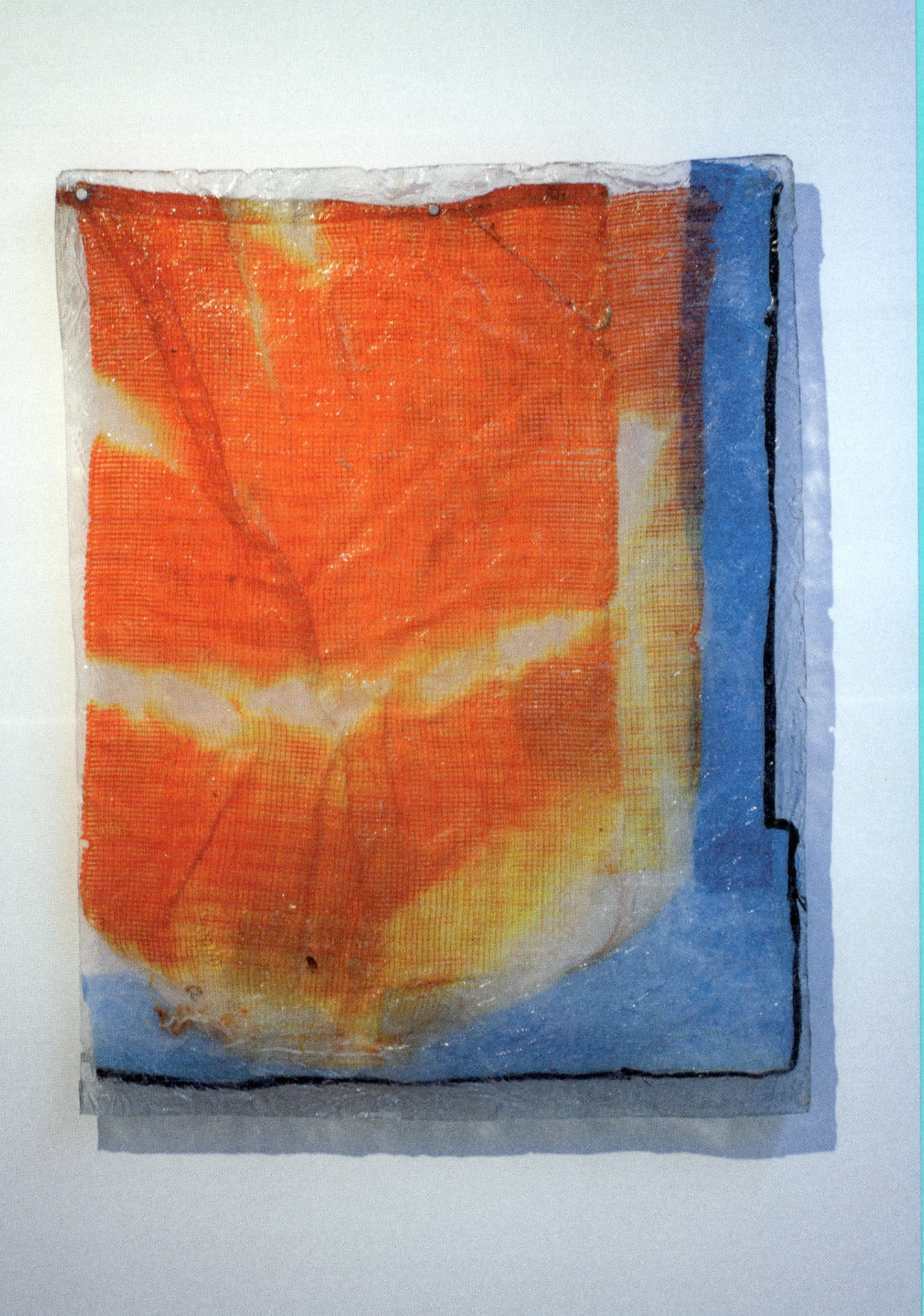

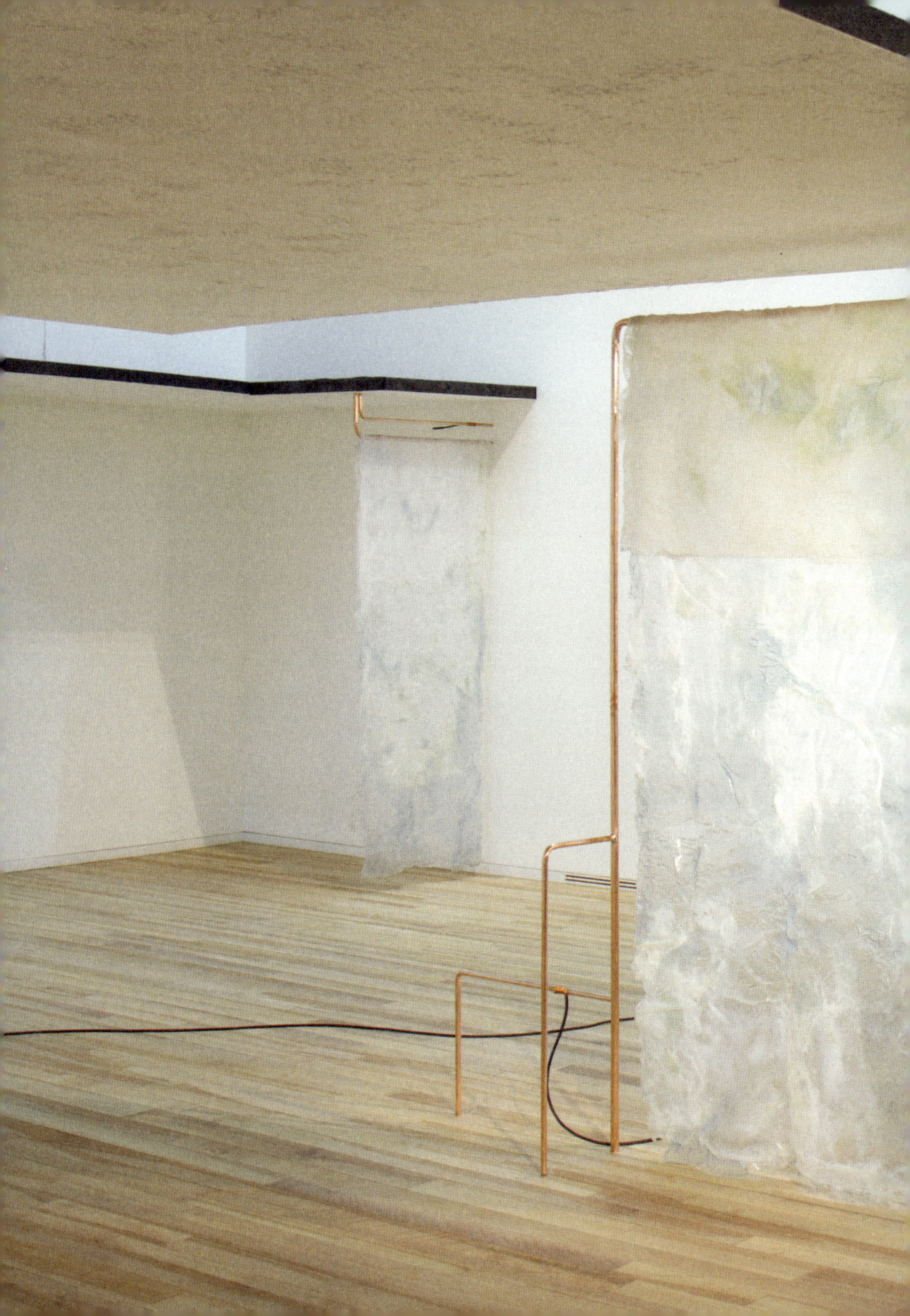

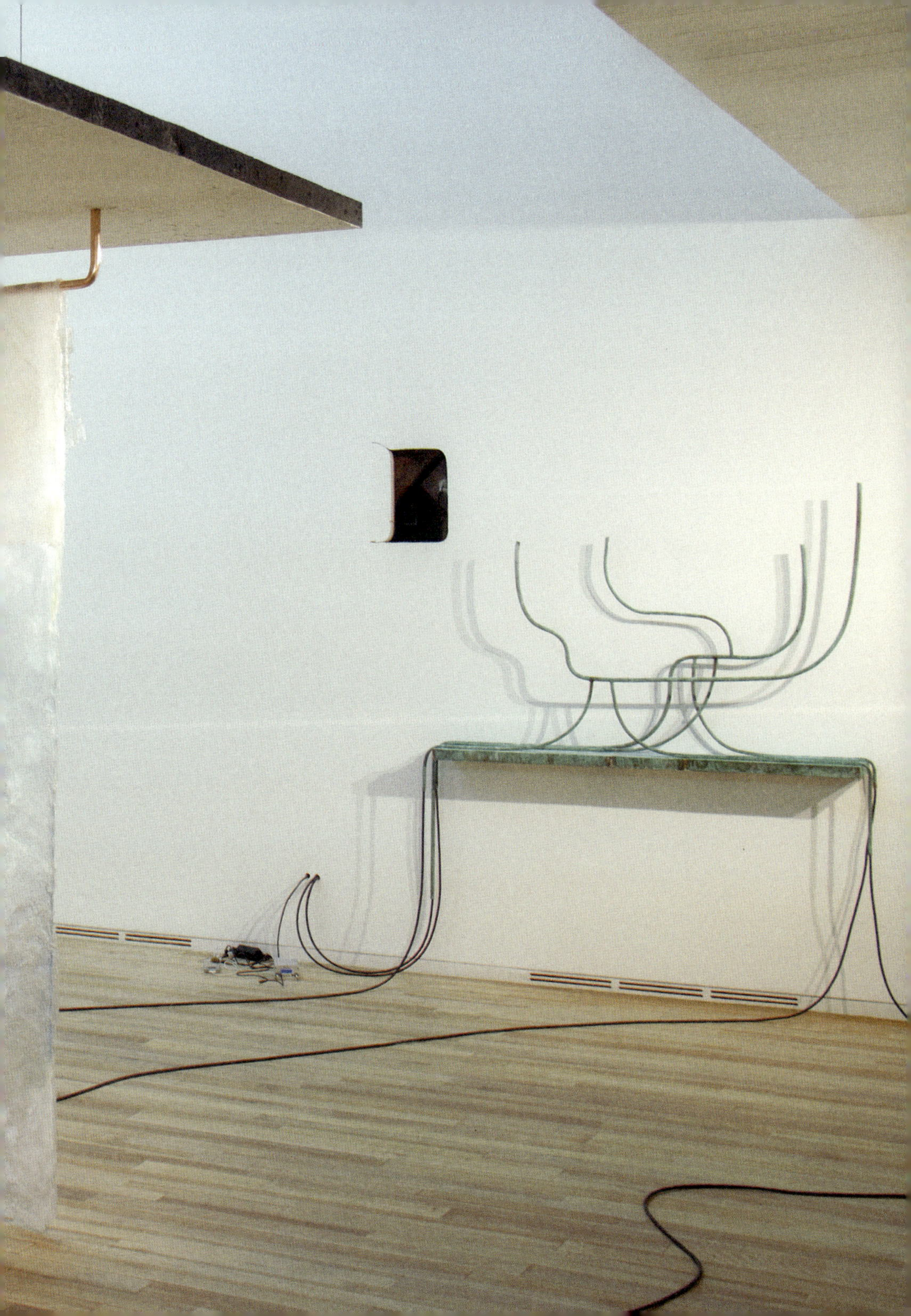

THE PROMISE
OF THE WAVES
ANNE FAUCHERET

> On the planking, on the ship's bulwarks, on the sea, with the course of the sun through the sky and the ship, an unreadable and wrenching script takes shape, takes shape and destroys itself at the same slow pace—shadows, spines, shafts of broken light refocused in the angles, the triangles of a fleeting geometry that yields to the shadow of the ocean waves. And then, unceasingly, lives again.
> —Marguerite Duras,
> *The North China Lover*[1]

1
Quoted as an epigraph in Félix Guattari, *Chaosmosis*, trans. Paul Bains and Julian Pefanis (Bloomington: Indiana University Press, 1995).

The imagery of modernism and its failures as well as its hybrid, popular appropriations, has characterized Wilfrid Almendra's work until now, but has left little tangible trace on his current output. The pacified ghost of modernism has given way to post-humanist demands. Almendra's projects are site-specific, both conceptually and physically, and he has a preference for spaces that, formally and historically, are atypical, heterodox, singular. He occupies them, and, above all else, sensitizes the visitor to the experience of this occupation.

In 2013, Almendra installed *L'Intranquillité* at Passerelle contemporary art centre, a former warehouse in Brest. In this work, a translucent structure with a rectangular ground plan occupies the central space. But a closer examination reveals that there are actually two structures. One of them has a perimeter of recycled glass sheets glued together. The second is suggested rather than fully realized, with just one wall in sheets of glass; the other sides consist of metal rods at a height of 2.3 metres, supported by three pillars, two in aluminum, the third in shuttered concrete, under the middle of the rod opposite the glass structure. This accentuates the airy, almost floating aspect of the installation. Between the two modules there is a passage, 60 cm wide, that cannot be entered, suggesting a space that is given over

2
This was not a random choice by Almendra. *Monstera deliciosa* is a popular domestic plant. In the wild, it proliferates rapidly and anarchically.

to rubbish or ruderal vegetation. It denotes the mandatory separation between houses. There is a profusion of ornamental plants—*Monstera deliciosa*[2]—that threaten to topple the walls. One of them has escaped from its confinement. By putting these plants in an intermediate space, an interstice, Almendra overturns ideas about the occupation of space, symbolically revitalizing non-places, no-man's-lands, wastelands. He celebrates natural entropy, whose rhythms he incorporates into the temporality of his work.

In 2014, at the asymmetrical art centre in Chelles, comprising two adjoining ancient churches that have been turned into a single space, Almendra came back to the idea of a natural, anthropic (and entropic) environment with *Between the Tree and Seeing It*, whose juxtaposed plates of recycled glass give a home, or a frame, to vegetation. But the ground plan is more complex, with the contours of a kitchen garden. And its mass overshadows the surrounding space. A variety of plants grow freely, as in an untended greenhouse. In the centre of the chapel there is *September 25th 2013 at night*, whose perfect white 29.28-square-metre ceiling, with its skylight, is suspended at a height of 2.5 metres. Visible in the background through three Gothic windows are 1970s residential blocks of the type whose presence in town centres is now much derided. In the exhibition space, a wooden table bearing different traces and inscriptions draws the eye towards the floor. According to one's viewpoint, it supports or presents a heavy copper plate that was cast collectively, and is unworked, almost crude. The force of the piece lies in a meeting between the evocation of a standardized space—private but transparent, empty—and a subtle though definite incorporation of usage and ritual, togetherness and collectiveness, into the space itself and the objects that occupy it. Potatoes made of aluminum are placed on the floor as if they had just been brought in from the garden. They recall those of Giuseppe Penone, but without the theatrical aspect of the faces printed as negatives. They were made with debris found in the aftermath of cyclone Xynthia on verandas in

Fos-sur-Mer, where permits had been handed out for construction in flood-prone areas. The piece speaks of non-monetary exchange, alternative economies, local culture, and transversal sociability. The final feature is a soundtrack that is audible within the exhibition space and also broadcast from there into the town every thirty minutes on FM frequencies belonging to mainstream radio stations—but for less than a minute each time, so that the source of the signal cannot be identified. It consists of poems in Portuguese declaimed in a slow, serious voice by their author, Jorge Armando Sousa, a stonemason Almendra met in Portugal while building a house there. This poet of the concrete and the everyday speaks of construction and occupation, (human) abandonment and (natural) reconquest. From the triviality of building sites, waste grounds, and materials, he extracts signs of a celestial community and an immanent link between all things.

SENSITIVE SPACES
In 2016, a year after completing a residency of several months with Fogo Island Arts, Almendra returned there to exhibit in a challenging space—a kind of well, seven metres deep, bathed in light (albeit electric), with a lower-ceilinged antechamber. Subtly oscillating between difference and repetition, he recovered certain preexisting elements or ideas, eschewing innovation in favour of the experimentation and collaborations which can spring up in given situations—and which are thus always new.

Light Boiled Like Liquid Soap is an immersive environment, not heavy but muffled. The spatial approach is delicate and economical but complex, combining vertical and horizontal markers, effects of opacity and transparency, closure and openness, light and shadow, broken lines and curves. Different occupational densities are created by configurations of flat volumes, planes and lines, in islets strewn across the space. Situated just inside the threshold of the gallery, a wooden platform suspended from slim metal cables intensifies the physical sense of confinement produced by the low entrance. But it is attenuated by the rest of the space, which is considerably higher, more airy and less dark, with two other platforms suspended at the same height. Covered in white plaster through which a fine metal grid (chicken wire) can be made out, these right-angle polygons suggest false, fragmented, incomplete ceilings. They lead the eye downward, showing signs of the manual work that shaped them, with variations of colour, marks of cuts and surfaces left visible; or rather, not masked. The horizontal structuring of the space, rigid and uniform, is softened by thick, translucent vertical silicone rectangles with ill-defined edges, hanging from one or more thin copper tubes attached to the suspended platforms and/or anchored in the floor or the wall. This network extends across the floor, where black electrical cables link the sculptural islets in graphic itineraries. The junctions are bound with covered copper wire. On the right-hand wall, a delicate skein of oxidized copper tubes supported by a shelf, also in copper, suggests a candelabra or an altar. On either side of the sculpture, copper tubes morph into electrical cables that descend to the ground, then join the network, or are inserted into the wall, where the origin of the configuration is presumably situated. A plaster-wrapped tube the diameter of a domestic water pipe runs from the entrance, at waist level, to a network of plaster-covered tubes some ten centimetres above the ground. On the wall, separate from the rest—both spatially and because it is the only object not connected by the electrical cables—is one pictorial work: a silicone inclusion of a red, orange, and blue plastic bag found on the seashore.

Apart from the touches of colour that can be seen here and there, like the green of the oxidized copper, it is black, white, and transparency that dominate. But this environment is characterized by filigree patterns: sculpture becomes drawing, material becomes flat. The emptiness created between the lines is inherent in the work. Dynamic and active, facilitating projection and connection, discontinuity and reversibility, this void gives a voice to things while also making possible an all-embracing approach to space, the occupation of which is not expressed in accumulation or utilization, but in the fragmentary, the precarious, the evanescent, the immaterial. The deliberate integration of shadows, and a radio connected to a smartphone, are further signs of a desire to disseminate the work while stopping short of its disappearance. The FM radio signal is indispensable but invisible, auditory but inaudible. It is a key to the work, elucidating the networked aesthetic, which also has a particular function, in that the conductive structure, pervading the environment and connecting it to the steel-framed building, creates a massive space of resonance and amplification. But the radio signal cannot be heard in the exhibition space. The artist has spatially separated the transmitter and the receivers so that the perception of the work is also fragmented. A displacement, or incursion, into the local social space is necessary if the sensorial experience is to be complete, above and beyond the discursive apprehension of the work.

The scales and dimensions of this installation implicitly relate to bodies. Along the wall, starting at the entrance, a plaster-wrapped tube at the same height as a dancer's barre orients and accompanies us, almost inviting us to lean on it as on a handrail. The adept arrangement of the different elements directs movement in space and distances of reception. At hand, in every sense, the piece invites us to palpate and to look through the body. Despite a discreet frugality and an aesthetic fragility, it is acted on by the environment. There is a slight disorientation of visual and spatial perception, a feeling of exiguity and volatility, concurrent strangeness and familiarity. References to habitat are numerous. All of the materials possess a strong power of evocation. Far from being specific to art, they mostly derive from other sectors: construction (wood, copper); medicine (silicone); or contemporary consumption, mobility, and communication (plastic bags and electrical cables). From the standard ceiling height of European social housing (2.3 metres) to the total area of the suspended elements, which is also that of the house where Almendra lived during his residency with Fogo Island Arts, via what looks like towel

rails (the copper tubes) or a decorated mantelpiece
(the copper shelf and the tubular metallic sculpture),
there are references, albeit abstract, to a familiar but
subterranean space of habitation. Rather than a living
room, this is a utility room, a basement, or an amateur
workshop. It is a refuge. And there are other, concomitant
indications of productive spatial occupation. Almendra
worked frequently in the exhibition space itself. And
this has left some traces, such as the incision in the wall
that reveals, along with the metal structure of the building, its nodal point—that of metal beams and tensile
forces. This is where he plugged in his transmitter. The
gallery becomes a space for life, and for work; for con-
templation and broadcasting. It is an intersection between
the private and the public, interiority and exteriority.
Fluid, unstable, porous, it is underpinned by circulation
and exchange. It gives a persistent impression of
being connected.

VIBRANT MATTER

It is through spatial organization, but also through the
methods and conditions of production and the nature and
treatment of materials, that Almendra orchestrates the
occupation of space and the orientation or evocation of
bodies, whether human or nonhuman, visible or invisible, desired or disappeared, incarnate or without organs.
The surfaces are shiny, matte, smooth or rough, expanded,
oxidized, burnt or polished. They look to be either new
or worn. They may suggest an epidermis, a roof, or a ban-
dage, but at any rate, almost always, a protective layer
that is at once an interface and a place for communication between the inside and the outside. Protection,
restoration, or indeed enhancement: these three significant approaches are reflected in the materials themselves.
Plaster evokes the immobilization of broken bones; silicone
brings to mind plastic surgery. And the omnipresent meta-
phor of a basement represents the idea of protection
and refuge. Paradoxically, however, the space is not hermetic, but permeable. It transmits and communicates
outward, like a skin. Some treatments stabilize materials,
like the use of a blowtorch to scorch the upper side of

the suspended wooden platforms, recalling the power of fire, which has ensured human survival and emancipation since time immemorial. Other treatments, including the uncontrolled oxidation of the copper and silicone, give free rein to molecular recompositions. The artist's fortuitous combination of two different silicones, for example, unexpectedly generated a runaway chemical reaction that he observes and conserves.

Letting go and experimenting, if always playfully—these are fundamental to Almendra's work, and they do not preclude fond attention to matter. It is not a question of mechanical or technological intervention, let alone outsourcing, but of a physical, attentive, sometimes repetitive, sometimes collective production process that brings together expertise and materiology. In contemporary art, over the last few years, the paradigm of artisanal activity has reappeared in the form of rigour, attitude, and production methods. Manual work is often highly visible. For Almendra, who has always embraced materials, with a predilection for the handmade, and who welcomes serendipity into his work, what counts is the structural, not the aesthetic; the political, not the cosmetic. He brings art back to vernacular practices, combining the work of the head with that of the hand, favouring experimentation, and slowing down the temporality of production. As he passes a blowtorch over the upper sides of the suspended wooden platforms, he is using a method of insulating and waterproofing roofs that ends with the application of tar. The hole that reveals the steel structure of the building, with the work-machine plugged into the architecture-machine, was made with a jigsaw in a trial-and-error search for the nodal point. The treatment and tools sometimes derive from a practical insight, a "poietic hybrid,"[3] as with the silicone, pressed by glass bottles and hardened by natural oxidation. Improvising on aesthetic canons and the supposed distinctions between "high" and "low," Almendra de-functionalizes (sometimes unceremoniously), then re-functionalizes, though without completely erasing, past biographies of materials and objects.

3
Richard Sennett, *The Craftsman* (New Haven: CT: Yale University Press, 2008).

Materials and/or objects enter into Almendra's work in different ways. He collects them during his various peregrinations, exchanges them, or purchases them on the open market. He is interested in local practices such as the use of wood in the construction of houses on Fogo Island; the removal of objects such as plastic bags from the usual cycle of production, consumption, and disposal; or their connection to a form of personal narration. He undermines "the taxonomic structure that defines the world of things, lumping some things together, discriminating between others, attaching meanings and values to these groupings, and providing a basis for rules and practices governing the circulation of these objects."[4] He densifies them, introducing them into a new symbolic form of circulation, and changing their primary status as commodities. "Objects are the way things appear to a subject—that is, either a name, an identity, a gestalt or stereotypical template. Things, on the other hand, [signal] the moment when the object becomes the Other, when the sardine can look back, when the mute idol speaks, when the subject experiences the object as uncanny and feels the need for what Foucault calls a 'metaphysics of the object,' or, more exactly, a metaphysics of that never objectifiable depth from which objects rise up toward our superficial knowledge."[5] Almendra is intrigued by things. He lets them act and express themselves.[6] As Roger Caillois put it:

I treat stone with deference, but as the insensible mineral that it is, and remains. I treat fables as fables, with the caution, uncertainty and incredulity they command. More than once, however, I have found myself thinking that stones should be seen as something like poems, and that fiction is where one should seek the perpetuity of stones, and their unshakeable signification, in other words, a way to reunify, however tenuously,

4
Arjun Appadurai, *The Social Life of Things: Commodities in Cultural Perspective* (Cambridge: Cambridge University Press, 1986).

5
W. J. T. Mitchell, *What Do Pictures Want? The Lives and Loves of Images* (Chicago: University of Chicago Press, 2005).

6
Francis Ponge, *Le parti pris des choses* (Paris: Éditions Gallimard, 1942).

7
Roger Caillois, *L'homme et le sacré* (Paris: Folio, 1950). Unless otherwise noted, all translations by John Doherty.

8
Steven Shaviro, "The Body of Capital," *Pinocchio Theory* (blog), June 20, 2008, http://www.shaviro.com/Blog/?p=641.

9
Bruno Latour, *L'espoir de Pandore: Pour une version réaliste de l'activité scientifique* (Paris: Éditions La Découverte, 2001).

the disjointed, contrasted parts of our indivisible universe.[7]

This is the metamorphosis that is being acted out in the floating, vibrant environment that vacillates between immobility and entropy, subjection and agency. To begin with, there are the aforementioned uncontrolled effects of combination, aging, and oxidation that Almendra authorizes. But there is also a spatial overflowing on the order of parasitism. The entire installation is grounded in the architectural space. The plaster-wrapped pipes descend to the floor as though their journey continues beyond their visibility; the electric wires are all connected to the steel structure of the building; the cables holding up the false ceilings are anchored in the real ceiling. And the architectural structure itself nurtures the work: without an antenna there is no signal, and the whole building is both amplifier and antenna. The poetry is transmitted by hacking into official airwaves. For Steven Shaviro, the model of "embodied subjectivity" has given way to a viral, or parasitic, model of subjectivity.[8] The body, with the addition of technological and media prostheses, is now co-extensive with its environment and territory—Deleuze's "becoming-animal." It takes on vital forces connected to the environment that sustains them. The organisms are collective and interdependent. This is a wholly resonating body, a "vascularized collective"[9] with different actors, human and nonhuman, in an unstable equilibrium of tensile forces, mass, oxidation, conduction. Macroscopically, immobility reigns. Microscopically, chemical and physical processes bear witness to the activity of matter, which seems to self-organize according to its own syntax, offering the world new equivalences and correspondences. More than an absurd poetic flight of fancy, *Light Boiled Like Liquid Soap*, which is both the title of the exhibition and its main component, suggests an alchemist's laboratory in which a new set of connections between things is being created.

An awareness that an artwork can be an ecosystem of interdependent elements, human and nonhuman, past and present, is to be found in this exhibition. But accretion does not just result from an "act of creation," as the aftermath of a generous human intention. It was already there. A fishing trip included the collection of the plastic bags that provide the material for a series of works, simply entitled *bags*, though of course they are more than that. The randomly combined silicones create strange iridescences. And even the human initiatives are not exclusively human. "The sentences of this book also emerged from the confederate agency of many striving macro- and micro-actants: from 'my' memories, intentions, contentions, intestinal bacteria, eyeglasses, and blood sugar, as well as from the plastic computer keyboard, the bird song from the open window, or the air or particulates in the room, to name only a few of the participants. What is at work here on the page is an animal-vegetable-mineral-sonority cluster with a particular degree and duration of power. What is at work here is what Deleuze and Guattari call an assemblage."[10] There is porosity, and constant exchange, between the organic and the mineral, between humans and things.

NOMADIC COMMUNITY

Light Boiled Like Liquid Soap is neither the brainchild of a demiurge nor an expression of its subjectivity, but the result of complex collective situations where encounters influenced, at least in part, the direction of the work. On Fogo Island, a meeting with a local architect involved with the Fogo Island Inn, where the gallery is located, led to the drilling of a hole in the wall in search for the steel node at the heart of the installation. And Jorge Armando Sousa's poems, played over the radio, were essential, as they are in Almendra's work as a whole. Rhythmic, sonorous, concrete, they turn building sites, work areas, no-man's-lands, and construction materials into a vibrant, lyrical, raw, rough universe:

10
Jane Bennett, *Vibrant Matter: A Political Ecology of Things* (Durham, NC: Duke University Press, 2009).

> *Entulho a céu aberto / Eu vi aqui bem de perto / Carcaças de frigorifico / Com plásticos a mistura / Lixo de cor diferente / Que infesta o ambiente / Composto que muito dura.*

(Open-air rubbish dump / on this earth I've seen / carcasses of fridges / in a mixture of plastics / multicoloured waste / invading the environment / compost that'll be here for some time.)[11]

In exchange for the poems, Sousa obtained a year's worth of olive oil pressed by Almendra, for whom the alternative economic reality of barter is crucial, along with the mobility of production sites and a remarkable economy of means. At the core of Almendra's work there is "symbolic exchange"[12] that is immediate, interpersonal, not subject to the challenges and aporia of social legitimation. The frenetic circulation of words, acts, and gifts stands in opposition to the immobilized time of the obstructed or unilateral exchanges on which power is based. For Jean Baudrillard, the poetic act is a symbolic exchange that offers "reversible dispersion," in contrast to cyberneticized culture. Here, it is the code that disperses, and, in the end, reestablishes freedom of symbolic circulation.

Walks, explorations, observations, drifts; attentiveness to the abandoned, the invisible, the inaudible; a rejection of methodological or formal systematization; hybridization of knowledge and know-how, poetics and aesthetics; nomadism, in life and production. As Rosi Braidotti writes, "The nomadism in question here refers to the kind of critical consciousness that resists settling into socially coded modes of thought and behaviour. The central issue at stake is the interconnectedness between identity, otherness, subjectivity and power. The nomadic subject combines coherence with mobility. It aims to rethink the subject-other relationship without reference to humanistic beliefs, without dualistic oppositions, linking instead body and mind in a new set of intensive and often intransitive transitions."[13] In relationships both to the cultural-economic space, temporality, the destination of work and authorship, Almendra foregrounds multiplicities of exchange, de-territorialization, nomadism, porosity,

11
Jorge Armando Sousa, unpublished typescript, 2013–14, translated from Portuguese by Catarina de Oliveira and Paul Figueira.

12
Jean Baudrillard, *L'échange symbolique et la mort* (Paris: Éditions Gallimard, 1976).

13
Rosi Braidotti, *Metamorphic Others and Nomadic Subjects* (Berlin: Tanya Leighton Gallery, 2014).

and malleability with regard to systematic, transparent decisions. He agrees with Frédéric Neyrat's view of the present age as one in which "every trajectory seems geo-localizable, where every knowledge must be situated and efficient, every obscurity cleared up, every real singularity suspect."[14] What Almendra develops in his work—echoing a personal, family history of migration and travel[15]—relates to Edouard Glissant's idea of "archipelagic thinking," which he contrasts with "continental thinking," involving system, manifesto, and hegemony:

> Another form of thinking is on the rise, which is more intuitive, more fragile, threatened but in accord with the chaos-world and its unpredictabilities, possibly based on the conquests of the human sciences, but derived from a vision of the poetic, and the imagination of the world.[16]

> It informs the imagination of peoples, and their diversified poetics, which in turn it transforms. Here, in other words, its risk is realized. [...] [Archipelagic] thinking outlines the imagination of the past: nascent knowledge. It cannot be halted for evaluation, or isolated for transmission. It is about sharing, which no one can deny, or, stopping, proclaim.[17]

This thinking is articulated within two concepts that fundamentally inform Almendra's work: opacity and relationship. Opacity is an epistemological concept that gives individuals the right to maintain a depth of shadow, a psycho-cultural depth, and non-transparency. Almendra's work retains its opacity: there is an obscure web of connections, and some decisions, both methodological and aesthetic, are not elucidated. The community of listeners is invisible, in the same way that the genealogy of certain pieces belongs solely to those who have contributed to

14
Frédéric Neyrat, *Atopias: Manifesto for a Radical Existentialism* (New York: Fordham University Press, 2017).

15
In his father's generation, this was marked by traumas of emigration, flight, and economic deprivation. What he took from it was the depth of working-class culture, multilingualism, and openness to the unknown.

16
Édouard Glissant, *Introduction à une poétique du divers* (Paris: Éditions Gallimard, 1996).

17
Édouard Glissant, *Poétique de la relation* (Paris: Éditions Gallimard, 1990).

them. Encounter, exchange, and, thus, relations engage in dialogues between different subjectivities, sensibilities, and forms of imagination. Without seeking to appropriate the Other, and a corresponding culture, Almendra cultivates hospitality and mutual interest. In preparing his 2017 exhibition at the Palais de Tokyo in Paris, he worked with visual artists Natacha Jouot, Tiziana La Melia, and Gareth Moore; New Orleans musician Mr. Quintron; and Le Berger, a Cameroonian hip-hop musician, thereby enlarging the creative community at the origin of the radio transmission. How, then, is one to enter into "the difficult complexion of a relational identity that comprises openness to others, without a risk of dilution?"[18] This is where the interplay between opacity and relationship takes place. Thanks to opacity, relationship can equally be open, contingent, and unpredictable. Glissant cites language and poetics, to which Almendra regularly refers. No language can claim universality. "The poetics of Relatedness requires all the world's languages. Not to know them, or meditate on them, but to know (to feel) that they exist with necessity. And that this existence decides on the accents of all writing."[19] Portuguese poetry is one such accent. The ontology of relationship, which implies "rhizome-identities" and nomadic communities, sets the seal on an imagination of relationships to a world in which each being—human or nonhuman—could express the world in its own language and act on the world in its own way. Imagination presides equally over poetic and political formulation.

*

Physically and conceptually rooted in architectural space, but also the biographical and local context, *Light Boiled Like Liquid Soap* constitutes a distinctive apparition, a discrete distortion—an *ex machina* machine. For Wilfrid Almendra, art is a non-productivist encounter between diverse subjectivities, temporalities, and realms, aside from any teleological consideration. He is less interested in critical manifestos than in the saboteur's disruptions, the orator's declamations, the poet's murmurings. His

[18]
Glissant, *Introduction à une Poétique du Divers.*

[19]
Ibid.

work is a political whisper that fluctuates between withdrawal and ostentation. It is a promise. The poetic voice conveyed by the appropriated transmission, as the final expressions of the sculptural system, was not in fact heard by very many people. And so much the better, because things appear to us only in terms of what they promise. They hold us in suspense, referring to an elsewhere, a future which, though emerging, is not yet fully present. Living, as Jacques Derrida said, means waiting for someone or something whose coming into being must exceed and surprise all predetermined anticipation.

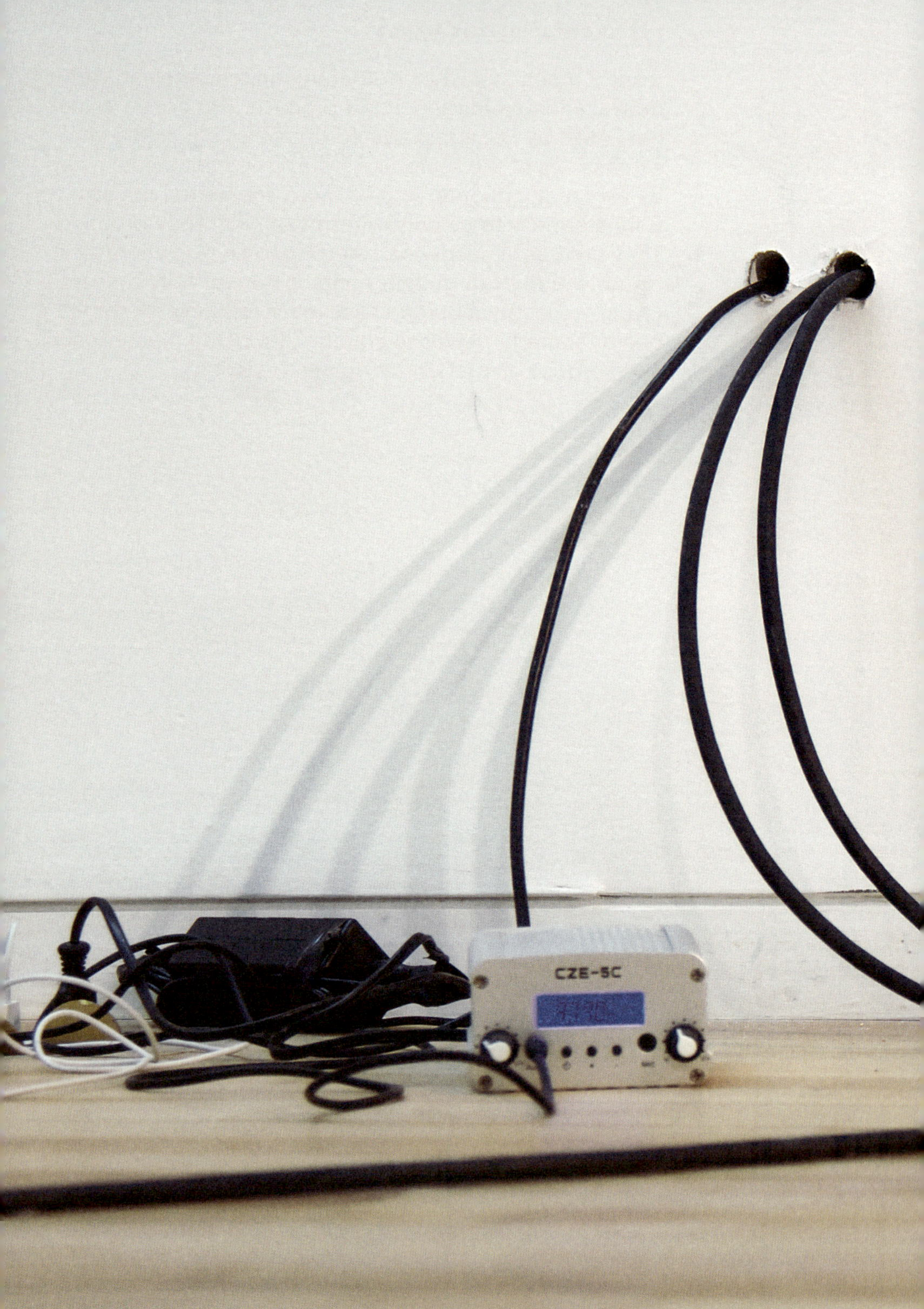

CZE-5C

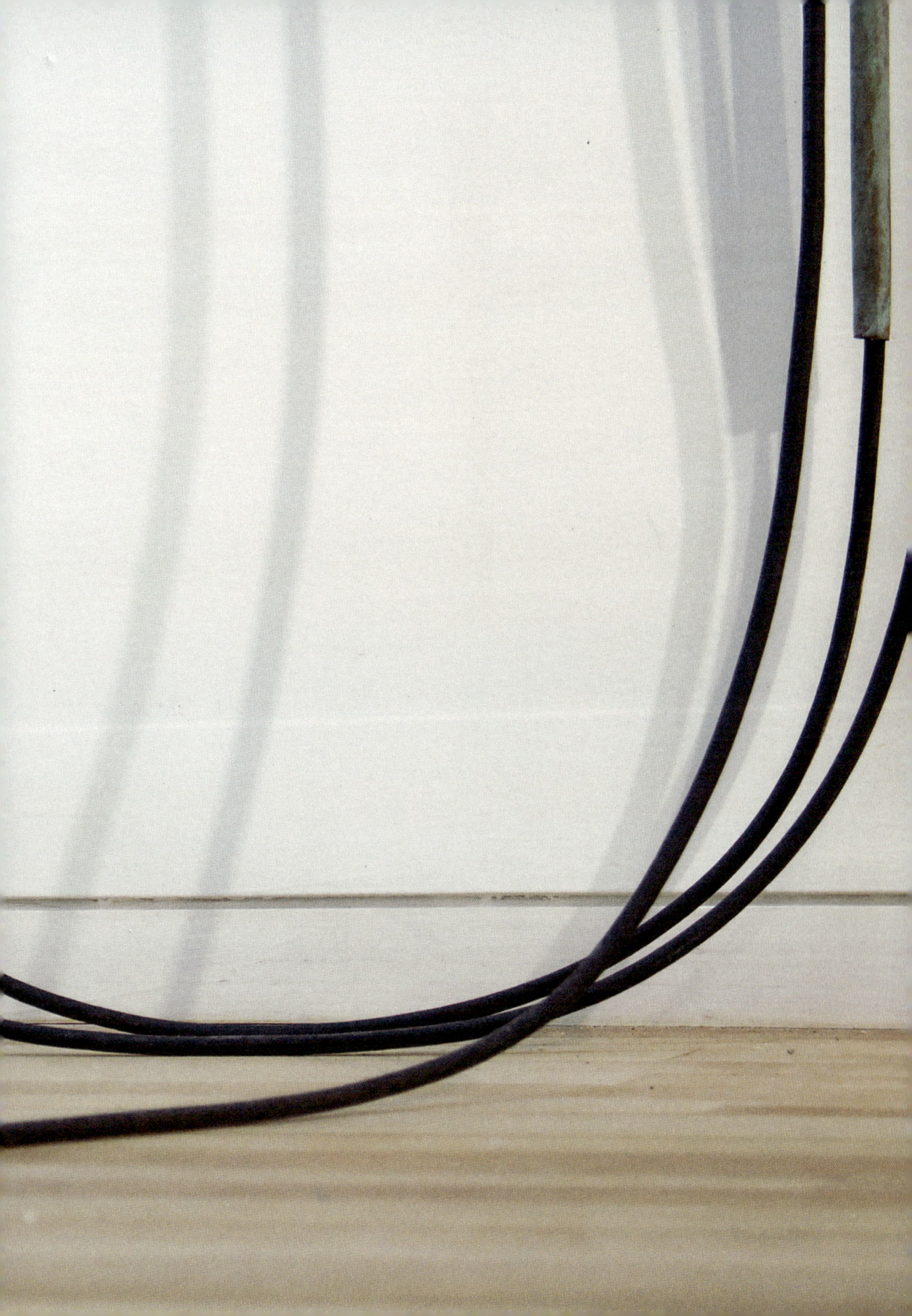

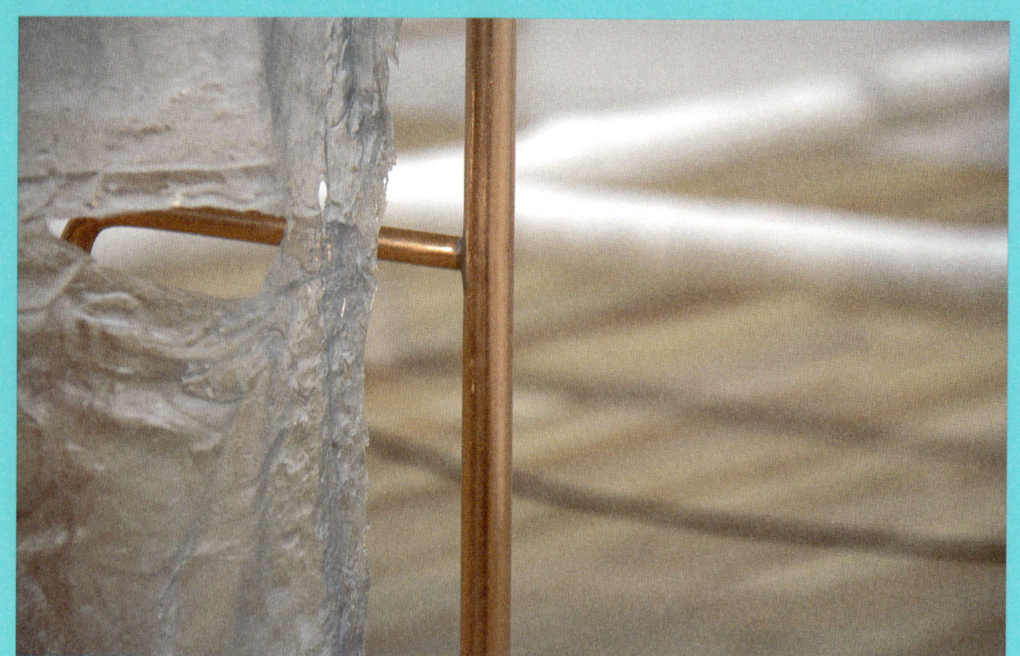

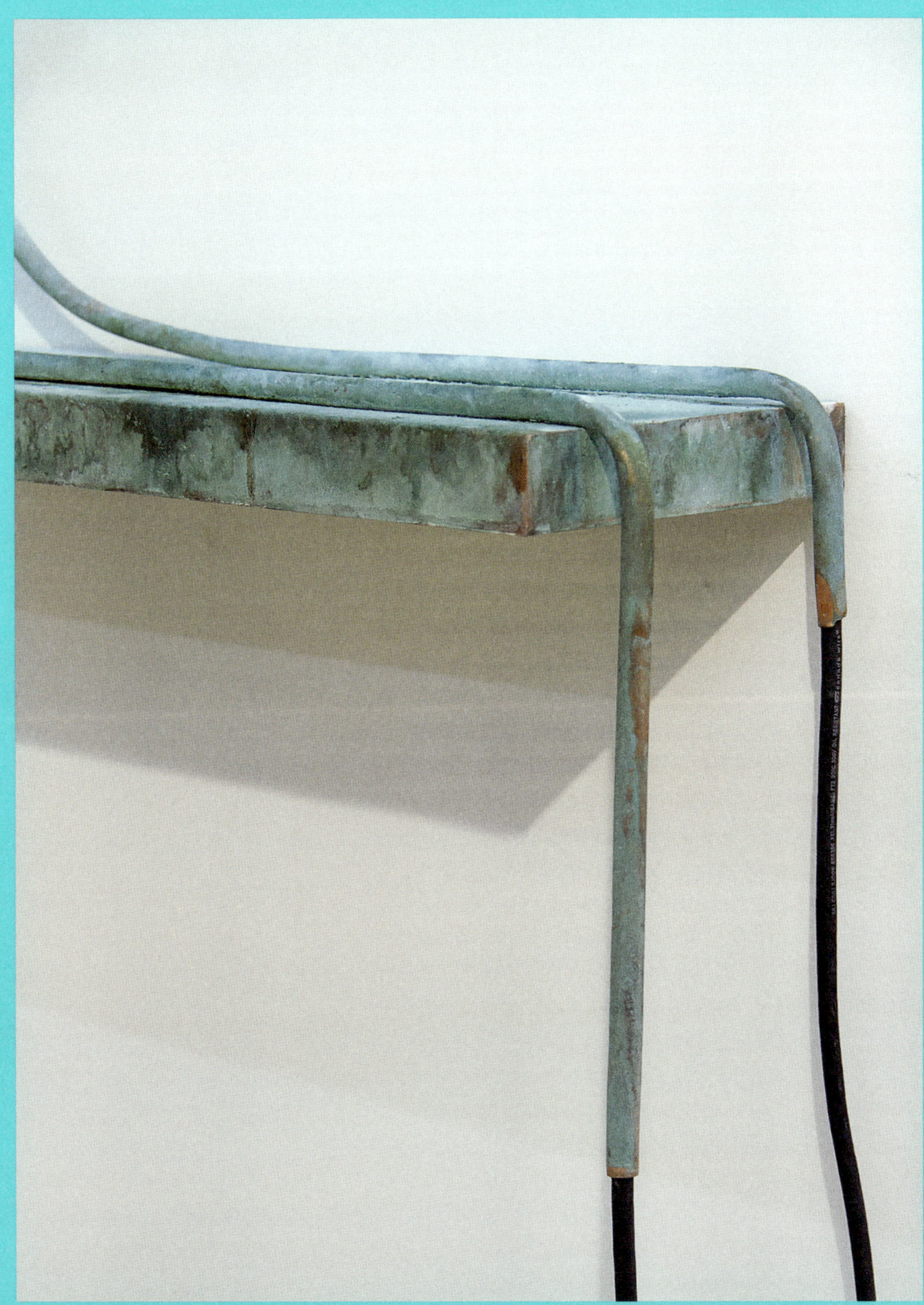

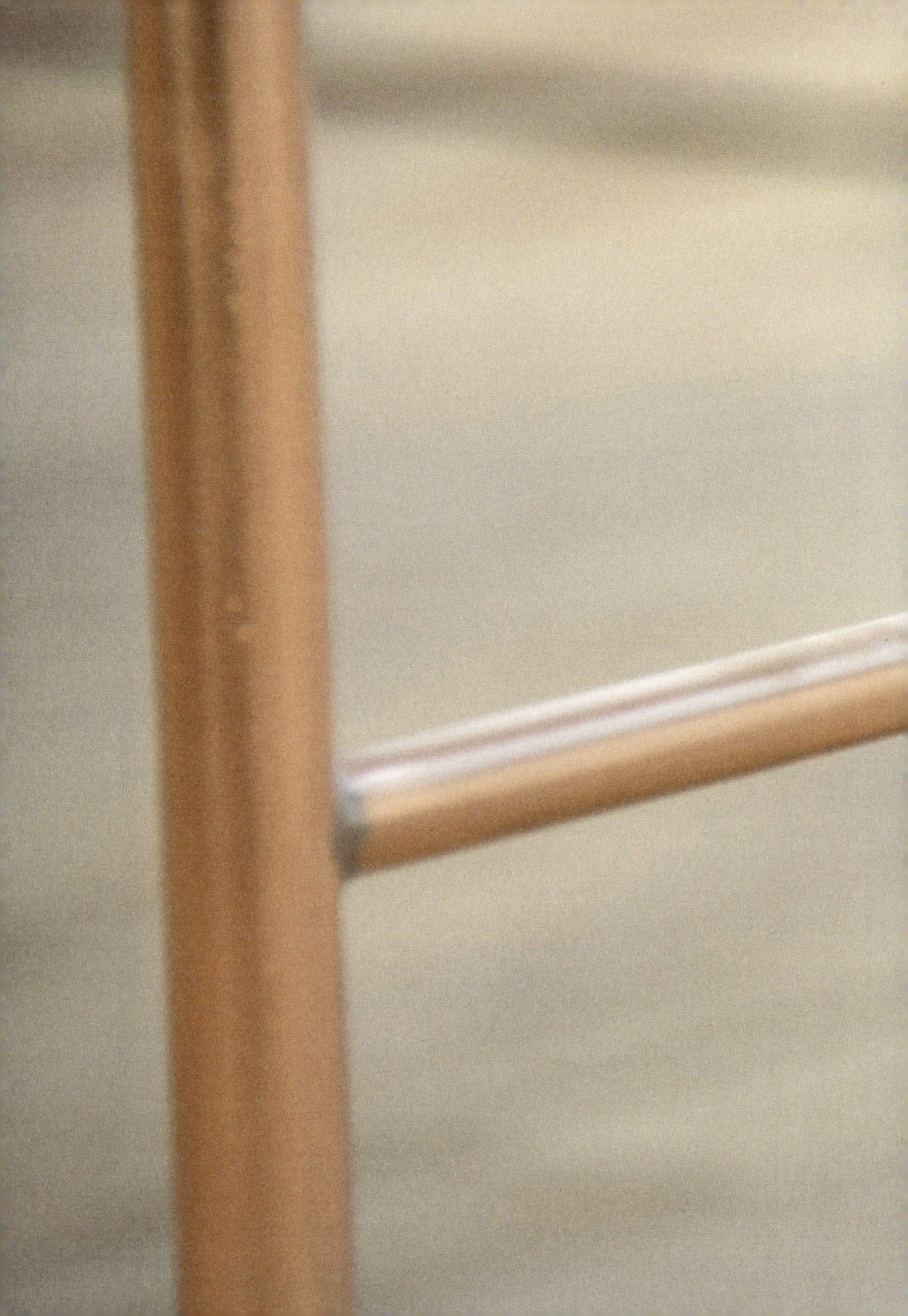

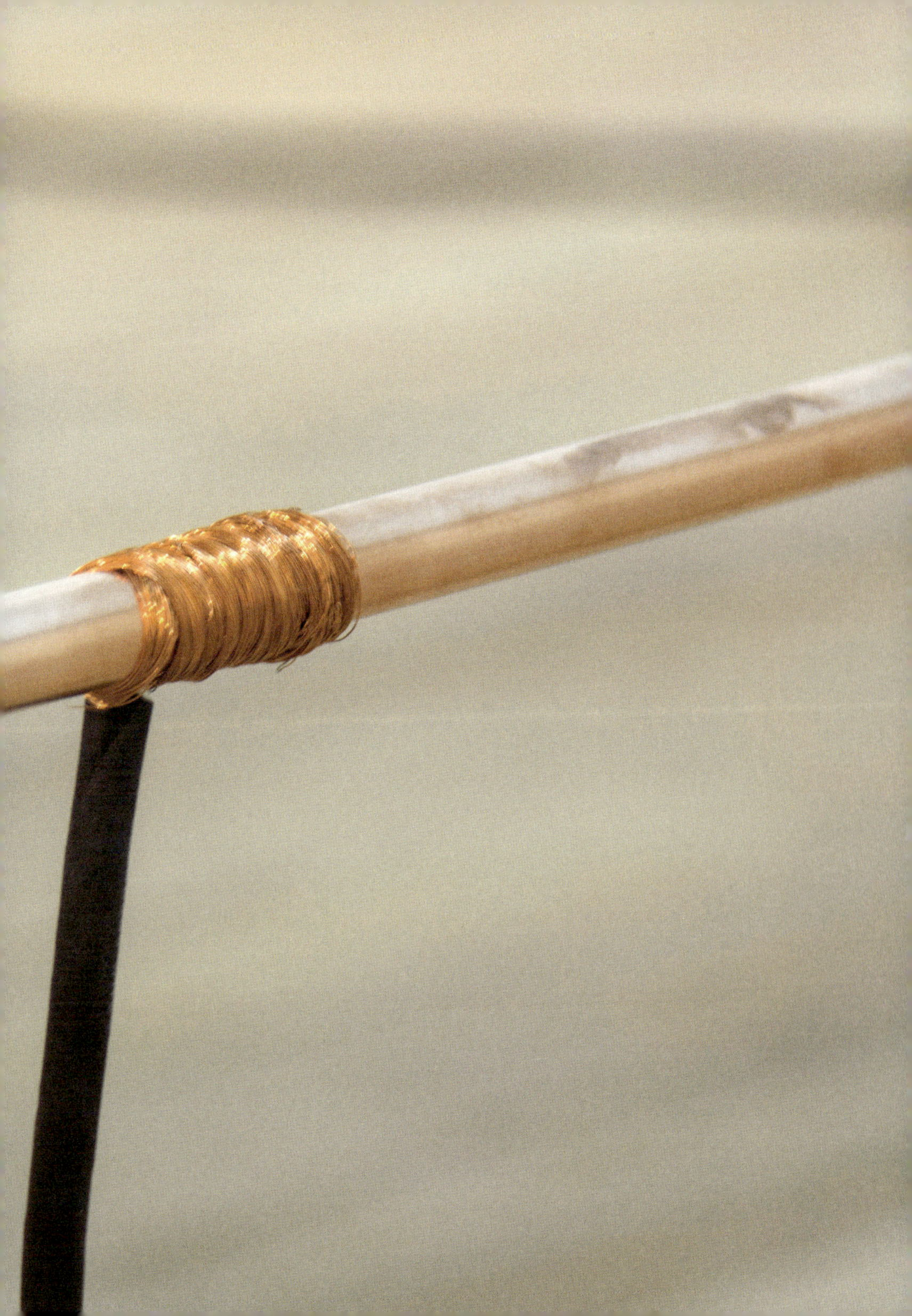

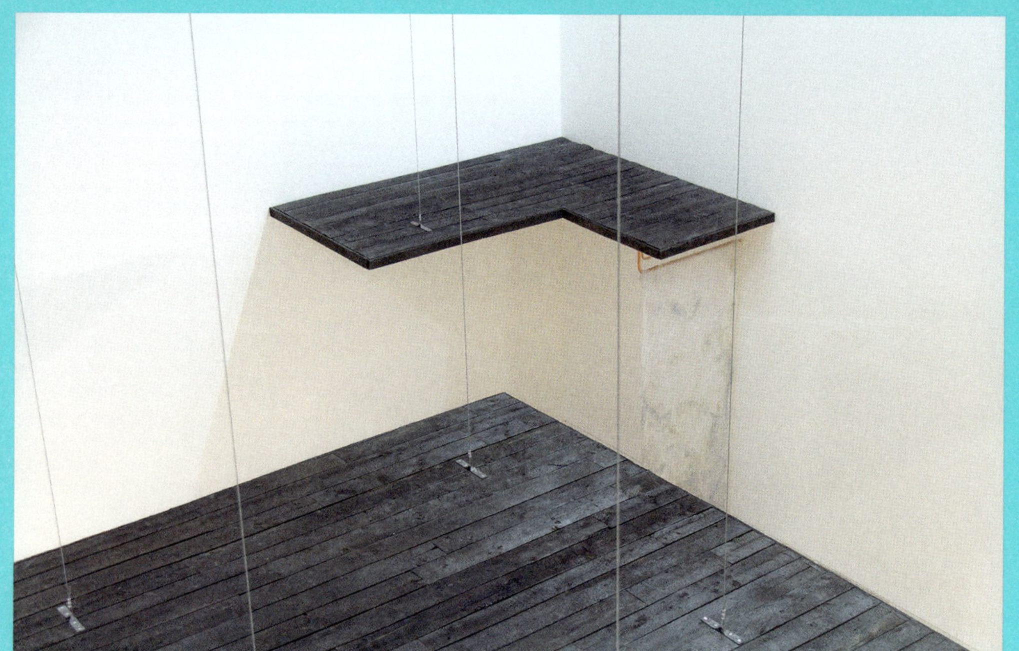

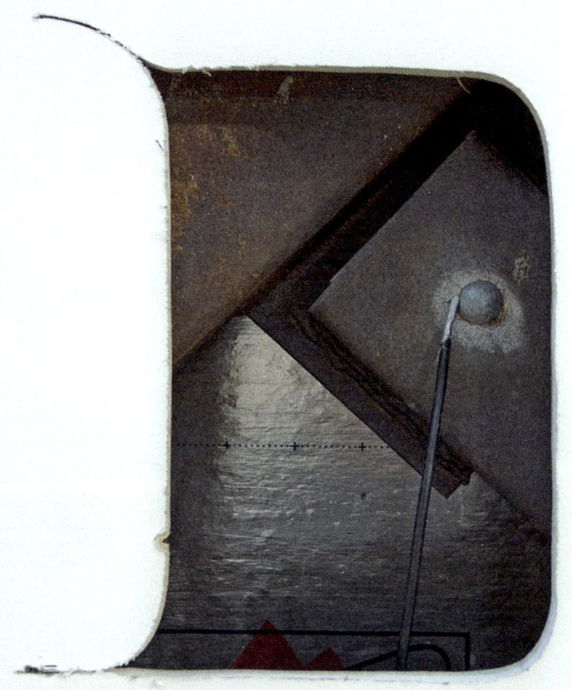

IT'S IN PERMEABILITY THAT THINGS PLAY OUT

WILFRID ALMENDRA IN CONVERSATION WITH ALEXANDRA MCINTOSH AND NICOLAUS SCHAFHAUSEN

ALEXANDRA MCINTOSH
Walking through *Light Boiled Like Liquid Soap* is an experience that moves beyond the visual into a more bodily, almost visceral form of perception. How do the materials and the arrangement of the space evoke and influence our physicality?

WILFRID ALMENDRA
In my work I often use ordinary materials that evoke everyday experience and individual desires or memories. For *Light Boiled Like Liquid Soap* (*LBLLS*), I used elements that occupy a modest position in our systems of value construction, such as plaster, electrical cables, copper pipes, screws, nails, wood, wire mesh, silicone, and staples. They're all around us (as Westerners, in any case). They structure our daily lives, our habitats, our zones of comfort or refuge. They're not remarkable or associated with artistic experience. They're there, in the installation, even before the visitor identifies them as an integral part of the work. There's a physical relation that's almost of the order of the preexistent. It comes through gradually as one moves around and takes the measure of the space. The immersion is not instantaneous: it builds up little by little through details and the way the space functions. The sign is diffuse. In effect, there's quite a sensual relation to materials and space.

I also play with standard measurements. As you enter the installation, there's nothing "spectacular, sculptural, centred" to be seen. It's quite casual: you're welcomed and embraced. You pass beneath a suspended platform without actually realizing that it's one of the components of the work. The rest of the building has high ceilings, whereas that of the space you pass through to begin with is of standard height. The norms that govern our bodies and experiences are such integral parts of our lives that they're invisible. But they're typologies that denote class phenomena. I wanted to play on a sort of sensorial déjà vu. Even if you don't live in public housing, your body recognizes this kind of space, whose modernist metrics are based on physical proportions. The height of the entrance is also a means of guiding the visitor into a place of possibility, the way you might go down into a cellar, into the bowels of an edifice. You're there where things are made, not in a space of representation. Whether it be the height of a ceiling or the strangeness of a copper pipe that ends up being observed, I wanted to create a combination of comfort and discomfort that would open up a breach in the order of the habitual, so that it might be possible to look at or feel things differently, without the certainty of a stable system where everything is in its place.

NICOLAUS SCHAFHAUSEN
You began with something known, then: something that derived from the history of sculpture, or of habitat.

W A
Yes, conventions like standard heights: objects placed at the level of a shelf, tubes at that of a dancer's barre. Here I'm trying to put it into words, but in fact it's simple and physical. The visitor's gestures and movements are matched by interlocking spaces, forms, opacities, and transparencies. Within the space itself, things are more intimate, and the inherent tensions mean that different details and materials become objects of attention. The installation functions as a whole, but there are also many discrete elements. My idea was that the configuration would be structured by the details themselves, which would anchor perception. For example, the electrical wires wound around the copper tubes and the exposed steel structure of the building are important. Ordinary things become active. I want the visitor to look for textures, which is why the experience is so tactile. Anyone who's been a dancer will be struck by the height of the tubes. In visual terms, they're also, simply, present in our homes. But here, they look like organs—orifices with fluid mechanics. The tension is partly due to the heavy platform ceilings, held up by fine cables. There's a relationship to danger and an obvious fragility, as with the electrical cables. This is a space of control and comfort, both mechanical and corporeal. Visceral. The silicone elements are sensual, with

a suggestion of skin, or of the medical world. I come
from a working-class background, where you learn
things by doing them. Gestures and the rituals of repetition and imitation are important to me. With this installation, beyond the visual, I was looking for a relationship
to sculpture that would represent a more haptic way
of producing knowledge. The copper and plaster tubes
speak of circulation, heat, flux, electricity, organs, but
also repaired limbs. So there's a dimension of "care,"
along with one of uncertainty and fragility.

A M
The installation as a whole embodies multiple binaries;
it is at once familiar and destabilizing, seductive and
repellent, transparent and opaque. Then there is the
evocation of spaces of retreat alongside a desire to
connect with the external world via radio transmission.
Could you speak about this play of opposites?

W A
For some years I've been thinking about, and working
towards, an eccentric, ambiguous form of sculpture
so as not to rely on a system of value production or hier-
archy that wouldn't reflect my standpoint, my life, or
the people I work with. The reality of human experience,
desire, and repression that inspires my activity is labile
and sometimes contradictory. It's a modest, unstable
reality, but no less strong for all that. My aim is to establish a non-authoritarian relationship to the object that
will give visibility to collaborative processes in which the
power of sculpture isn't embodied in finished, immut-
able forms alone, but in something unregulated, diffu-
sive, active. Something that's at work. The material world
itself is caught up in cycles of creation and destruction,
complicated by toxicity and non-recyclability. In *LBLLS*,
this ambiguity is exemplified by the presence of elements that can be seen as existing in opposition. If, at
a certain point, something fixed or authoritarian is
observed, it's often unbalanced and endangered. There
are delicate issues. And I like this paradox. In the installation, things are placed more or less like garments and

everything could collapse, whereas elsewhere, elements of the framework, like the suspended platforms, seem hard and solid. Beyond binary relations, what interests me, essentially, is the indeterminate middle, which is neither one thing nor the other—a zone of encounters and possibilities where categories dissolve. And it's this precise place of desire and emancipation that I want to locate.

But to come back to *LBLLS*, yes, my aim was to create a paradoxical space. My point of departure was the way in which we inhabit the world and our relation to materiality as a vehicle for our desires, with the instrumentalization and ambiguity entailed by capitalism—consumption as an end in itself, a religion. Among the things on which our relationship to the environment and our capacity for togetherness are founded are energy and the home, in the sense of a habitat—a place around a fire, and food on the table. The way this is organized is political. It's clear, nowadays, in a time of energy transition, that such questions generate fear. Psychologically, the home is a place of safety and shelter. When you enter *LBLLS*, you realize that you've passed through a transitional zone in which your body was constrained. When you look upward, the ceilings are like suspended plaster monochromes that crush and contradict the historical avant-garde idea of autonomy or purity. Yet these forms aren't divorced from everyday reality, given that they represent the ground plan of the house where I was living on Fogo Island. Chicken wire covers the smooth white surface. It's hostile, by definition, but not actually dangerous. Not military. It's the kind of thing you might find in a garden or hen-house. There's even something domestic and reassuring about it, unlike global circulations, if in a clearly questionable way. The upper surfaces of the platforms are blackened and scorched, in a subliminal echo of the island's name—in Portuguese, "fogo" means "fire."

N S
So there are multiple elements that ground the installation in the everyday. These blackened surfaces—from
the second-floor window that provides a view onto the
installation from above, you see only blackness; inside,
you have light. Which brings us to the title of the installation. Can you speak about this?

W A
Yes, in effect, the view of the installation from above is
one of opacity, an "underground," or a "safe space." Then
there is an idea of translucidity, matter, softness, air. And
then, of course, there's soap, which brings to mind the
indulgence of bathrooms, but also the control of bodies.
We're between material and air, solid, gel. The installation
is traversed by two types of tube, in copper and plaster.
The circulation of water and heat. These are flows of survival. In an environment as hostile as that of Fogo Island,
heat is essential. And the plaster tubes are associated with
the heat of the boiler below ground, or the question of
waste materials, which, for me, is important. The floating
ceilings are made of wood recovered from a garbage
dump on the island. This recalls the idea of cycles, and
an economy, or a history of art, that goes back to Van Gogh
and Millet's gleaners: poverty. The pipes are rough and
ready; they've been repaired. It's not Duchamp's urinal
that interests me here, but rather an idea of circulation
and flow. Copper denotes electricity and conduction,
heat and cold. It's comfort and communication, like the
telephone. But also death. It means invisible circulation,
and force in a form that's solid and opaque. For some
time, from a conceptual point of view, I've been interested
in transparency and opacity and what they've meant,
historically, in terms of value, purity, and religiousness.
But at the same time, opacity is what you don't look at,
and what's protected from mainstream rules and hier-
archies. With this installation, you're not just in a refuge,
but also in a space whose perimeter is totally porous,
not at all hermetic. It's in permeability that things play
out, and in a psychological space between the two,
without well-defined contours. This is a precondition for

emancipation, when things dissolve into light and shadow. Purity's never present.

On the copper pipes, there are sheets of silicone. They look nice, and you want to touch them, but at the same time they're gelatinous and repellent. I use two kinds of silicone. One of them has applications in medicine, the other in construction, to make watertight joints. Strange to say, but they're mutually antagonistic. Their combination is toxic. So the crystalline, attractive character of the silicone is blurred, like a tumour, as with sfumato in painting. This toxicity creates colours and matter, as though it were alive. Which is paradoxical, in that there's nothing more synthetic than silicone. It's an example of the desire for de-centring that marks my work. I've always used silicone—but functionally, as a way of making things solid, so that in its surface there's just softness and material knowledge, bizarre and artificially toxic. Apart from the use of silicone in construction and medicine, silicon itself is used to make microchips. All of which participates in the accumulation of flows and capital that characterizes modernity.

AM

You've used the word "flux"—in the sense of continuous change and a cycle of exchange—in relation to the exhibition. What elements or ideas are in flux here?

WA

As I've said, the entire installation, with its visceral aspect and its tubing, suggests flux. And there are fluids ... The blue oxidation of the copper tubes, which is quite attractive, was actually obtained by urinating on them. In this installation, questions of circulation go beyond representation as such. Behind the form, my intention was that there should be an active force, and that the sculpture should operate in an invisible way. The components are interlinked, and the installation is literally an antenna. Conductors such as copper and steel connect to the structure of the building and to a radio transmitter. The installation is functional, sending out a signal over a distance of two to three kilometres. So there's a content that goes beyond the visible surfaces and forms.

N S
This signal, the radio transmission, is itself based on another form of exchange. Can you speak about your collaboration with the author of poems that were broadcast?

W A
This is the first time I've given full scope to an idea that actually arose some years ago. I was working at a construction site in Portugal when, at the end of the day, as we were hosing down a concrete mixer, a stonemason friend called Jorge Armando Sousa unexpectedly began reciting poetry. Afterwards, we talked at length, and I suggested that we do something together, not really knowing what might come of the idea. Jorge wrote poems—not about my work, but about our conversations, and subjects like his relationship to landscapes and to labour, to change and life situations, his membership in a sedentary Roma community ... He gave me a set of twenty poems, and in exchange I gave him the olive oil I'd pressed that year. Such encounters have always been present, and important, in my work. But they'd previously been hidden, buried beneath forms. I wanted to display our collaboration, and Jorge's poems. The question was complex. How do you integrate work like this into an economy of art, a world that's not your own? I didn't want to exploit or appropriate the content. The idea of incorporating Jorge's work into an exhibition gave me the impression that I'd be confining his words, halting their movement and cancelling out their agency. His poetry is secret and delicate, but also powerful. He writes his texts at night and doesn't show them to many people. What was needed was a place, and a form of existence, that would be faithful to his work—a content that would really exist in a space of freedom, not one of professional use. The ethical question became central, and I thought about the kind of form that would suit his voice. I finally just invited him to recite his poems, so that they'd be heard rather

than read silently. To record him, and to disseminate his voice on radio waves, seemed like the closest thing to the beautifully elusive quality of his work. Orality is important in his community. It's also something that interests me personally, and I wanted to respect it. In the end, given the presence of the transmitter in the installation, my sculptures are at the service of this content, which goes beyond a specific location, insinuating itself into Fogo Island's mainstream radio waves. Jorge's voice can be heard regularly, several times a day, unannounced, amid the normal programming and pop music, in homes, in shops, on boats sailing by ... More than an image arriving from elsewhere, what circulates is the power of his voice and imagination, reinforced by our discussions.

A M
This form of collaboration has continued in your work, and this project in particular continued to evolve beyond its Fogo Island presentation.

W A
Yes, that's right. Fogo Island has few radio stations, but at the Palais de Tokyo, in Paris, where the project took an augmented form, we developed an algorithm that allowed the content to be broadcast on random wavelengths at various times; I didn't want to intrude into the transmission process. And I continue to work on content through other encounters—recently, for example, with a Cameroonian musician known as "the Shepherd," who developed his practice by playing music to his flock on instruments he made himself. People like this don't need recognition in order to shine. It's what Fred Moten and Stefano Harney talk about in *The Undercommons*. The content exists in audio format, but also in exchanges. It's an economic form based on mutual assistance and gifts, a space of enrichment and friendship. Jorge's a member of a community of comings and goings, with sharings of expertise and stories about what's produced, which may be "elusive," but which are structural for me. And the pirate broadcasts create a fabric of relations within this invisible community.

NS

Radio has of course been extremely important for Fogo Island historically, both in its technological evolution and as a source of connection to the rest of the world. But there are other links between Fogo Island and Portugal specifically. Could you speak about these?

WA

For Fogo Island, I selected nine of Jorge's poems that evoke the landscapes of northern Portugal, with their mimosa and open-air garbage dumps. In a way, this resonates with the colonial history of the island, whose name was likely given to it by Portuguese fishermen at the start of the sixteenth century, probably as a reference to fires lit by the Beothuk, an Indigenous population who subsequently died out. It's strange to think about connections between territories whose realities and landscapes are so far apart, but which share so much history of conquest and resource exploitation. Despite the isolation you might feel on Fogo Island, these territories are connected to other places by the realities of exchange and commerce. It's like what I was thinking about with *LBLLS*. Newfoundland has been significant in the history of communication technology, given that the first undersea transatlantic cable, laid in the mid-nineteenth century, started out from Heart's Content. Fogo Island was also important for radio experiments and wireless communication: Guglielmo Marconi demonstrated the possibility of transatlantic communication with the station he installed there at the start of the twentieth century. And the island was opened up by the possibility of information and alerts being broadcast between communities and ships. It was a godsend for fishermen. I'm interested in the idea of air as a shared space, whereas in fact it's also subject to privatizations and circulations, both global and commercial.

AM

What about the stand-alone piece entitled simply *bag*? This for me connects very directly to global economies of exchange.

WA

Yes, the bag refers to the island's connection with international trade. I should mention that when I went fishing, all I pulled out of the water was this woven plastic bag, a waste product of the global economy that arrived there along international trade routes, probably having transported a commodity such as grain. In other words, it makes no sense to fantasize about pristine nature. Plastic is everywhere. And in food packaging it's universal, with a rhetoric based on hygiene and the emancipation of women. But all of it, once discarded, disappears from our visual environment.

AM

In addition, once encased in silicone, the bag becomes a kind of rarefied object, one that is inscribed within the language of art and thus another circulation system: the art market.

WA

Yes, absolutely.

NS

The exhibition as well as the texts in this publication exemplify the problematics of connection and exchange. Geographically and culturally, there are vast distances between Fogo Island and Marseille, Vienna, and Delhi, where you, Anne Faucheret, and Nicolas Idier are based, respectively. That distance is bridged almost instantaneously via technology, but it is a tenuous connection where interaction can be diminished or confused. What does it mean for you to attempt these connections in your work despite their fragility?

WA

I appreciate Nicolas Idier's work as a novelist, and I asked him to write something about the exhibition. We discussed the possibility, and the form it might take, which of course wasn't self-evident, seen from Delhi. He got involved at an early stage and asked me to send him as much material as possible, so as to shrink the geographical distance between us, and to give him an understanding of what I was doing on Fogo Island: the artistic process. But for me, in the heat of the action, this form of communication was unsatisfactory. To find words that would communicate what I was doing—it would've meant distancing myself from the work in order to apprehend it. I finally did something a bit strange. I set up a camera in the exhibition space so that Nicolas could see for himself the forms I was making, without our needing to talk to each other. It went out live on Internet sites that featured all sorts of weird and wonderful stuff. Nicolas could access it at any time, whether or not I was actually there. Though I forgot about its presence, he himself found it disappointing. He felt uneasy about being in the position of a voyeur, both conceptually and in real terms. It led, in fact, to something like the opposite of a connection. It emphasized distance; looking at a different reality from elsewhere, on a computer screen, at another time of day, but without being able to talk to the other person, or to say "Hello, here I am." And then again, either nothing interesting would happen or else Nicolas would be in front of his screen at a time that was awkward for me, like when one of the platforms was being installed. He found it galling to be unable to engage in communication, or anything else. An isolated witness. I suppose he was disconcerted by the distance and detachment. At any rate, that's what he said. In the end, his text wasn't an illustration of my work, but a result of a given situation, and his projection of it, as a writer of fiction. Which was much better. Connections may be simplified by technology, but this is not yet the general rule, and there's no reduction of distances, divergences, or fragilities. More generally, I'm interested in insular isolation and communicational interruptions, because they make it possible, paradoxically, to invent ways and means of maintaining and reinforcing existing connections. And itinerancy brings other possibilities to light ... I think that Anne, who made the trip to Fogo Island, also saw the situation as being special, and she created a space of experimentation that can be seen in her text.

A M
Coming back to processes of collaboration in your work, establishing relationships with local makers and tradespeople, is this something driven by necessity or do you seek out and draw influence from such contact?

W A
Apart from the radio work I've mentioned, my approach has always been structured by collaborations. Nothing heroic. They're a way of finding out how to do things— a kind of curiosity. I've always worked collaboratively. There's often been a sculpture, an object made by hand because I couldn't afford to pay people; in fact, I wouldn't have wanted to. It was the process, essentially, that interested me. Making a sculpture was often an excuse to knock on people's doors and talk to them about techniques and expertise, to ask questions that changed habits. With artisans, or non-artisans, I never have a worked-out idea or plan. I prefer to leave room for encounters, so that our respective skills and knowledge can form a point of departure for discussion and experimentation. This doesn't always work. Talented people have to be open to dialogue. I don't impose anything, or feel I'm owed anything. But if you take an interest in people's work, and spend some time doing so, in general there are stories and skills that come out. It has a lot to do with generosity and confidence and sharing. What's certain is that collaborations are integral to my sculptures. There are invisible but operative forces that partly define the visible, aesthetic experience of my work. This process, founded on encounters and mediations, has become increasingly important in recent years. I try to bring it to the surface, but I guess I'm unusual in the art world, and for a long time I kept it to myself. Which is why, more recently, I've been concentrating on installations, with circulations and the kinds of exchange that generate forms. As I think I've already said, I reflect on my work and its hierarchical relation to the art world, but also, at an individual level, the people around me, whose voices and actions are important to me.

N S
Is this motivated by an interest in the amateur or auto-
didact? Or perhaps by a desire to move beyond the
parameters of institutional frameworks and knowledge,
to inhabit spaces beyond standard economic systems?

W A
The stories and presences, but also actions and expertise,
found in my work often derive from people I've encoun-
tered quite by chance. What they have in common is a
certain experience of precariousness. Above all, they
develop alternative forms and practices that exist invisibly
and (both metaphorically and literally) like "garage practices." I admire their view of the world and wouldn't just
treat them as subjects or bind their actions to a rigid system of identification. In any case, I'm not in a position of
superiority. We talk. Sometimes we swap things. It's a bal-
anced relationship. When I mention "garage practices,"
I'm referring more to my own experience than to a critique
of institutional art. My purpose isn't to criticize the institution. As a child, I spent a lot of time in basements. My
father left Portugal on foot, as a minor, and he arrived in
France with no papers. He made his home there and
became a legal immigrant. He set up a business delivering
heating oil, and I helped him. I soon realized that places
had things to say. A garage could be a workshop, or a
storehouse for objects of emotional value that people
didn't want to throw away. It wasn't like a frigid underground environment, but a source of heat for the house-
hold. And all the tubes in the exhibition have a signifi-
cance for me—something on the order of "care." A garage
could be a place to repair things, to produce heat ... I put
in a lot of big, heavy tubes to bring people heat. But to
come back to your question, it's not so much that I'm
interested in amateurs or autodidacts. That's how I view
myself, even though, within the art world's system of
identification, I'm seen as a sculptor. It's true that I've produced numerous objects of formal complexity and aesthetics which express my relationship to work, labour,
and the pleasure of "doing it myself." The idea of "doing"
has always been important to me. It implies a direct

connection to matter, knowledge, and possible displacements of forms, or their transcendence. It's also an emancipation from standard things and forms.

A M
Would you say there is a political dimension to your work?

W A
I'm glad you asked me about this. Of course it's political. The technical tour de force aspect that characterizes many of the pieces might be seen as a gendered marker, like a claim to a sort of masculinity in which gestures are demonstrative and intense. But for me, it's never that. My work asks questions about masculinity, class, and conventions. There's delicacy in the actions and stories that are present in my work, if not necessarily in my working-class background. I play with codes. I think about my relationship to labour, and my milieu. There's an intense relationship to pain; you have to work hard to create value. Intellectual or creative activity isn't work if it can't be seen in terms of movements, energy, hours. You have to produce. Bodies have to be fit, actions effective. A lot of masculinity is invested in processes of validation and confidence building, but things can get fragile and tenuous. Instabilities and questionings are ever-present in my work. Apart from mastering (and thus controlling) the forms I create, I look to what I don't know, and I seek out people who can assist me. The transmission of expertise is essential to the constitution of a community, and it's often by deeds rather than words that we communicate. The production of an object can bring about encounters and activate the kind of alternative economies of mutual assistance that I talked about earlier. To conclude, it's clear that heating oil, or the energy question in general, is a central issue. Political divisions, fears, and denials create divisions between urban and rural populations. After decades of neoliberal politics, it's important to look at the less affluent classes from a social, aspirational, or even aesthetic viewpoint. Personally, I want to create forms that reflect these questions with subtlety, and also, I hope, a little poetry.

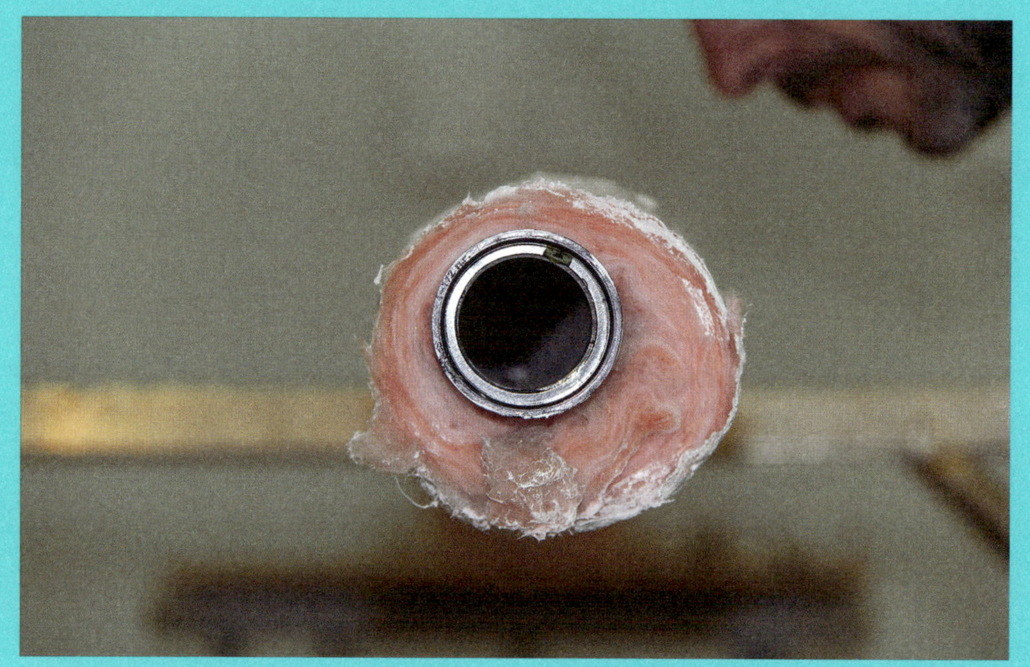

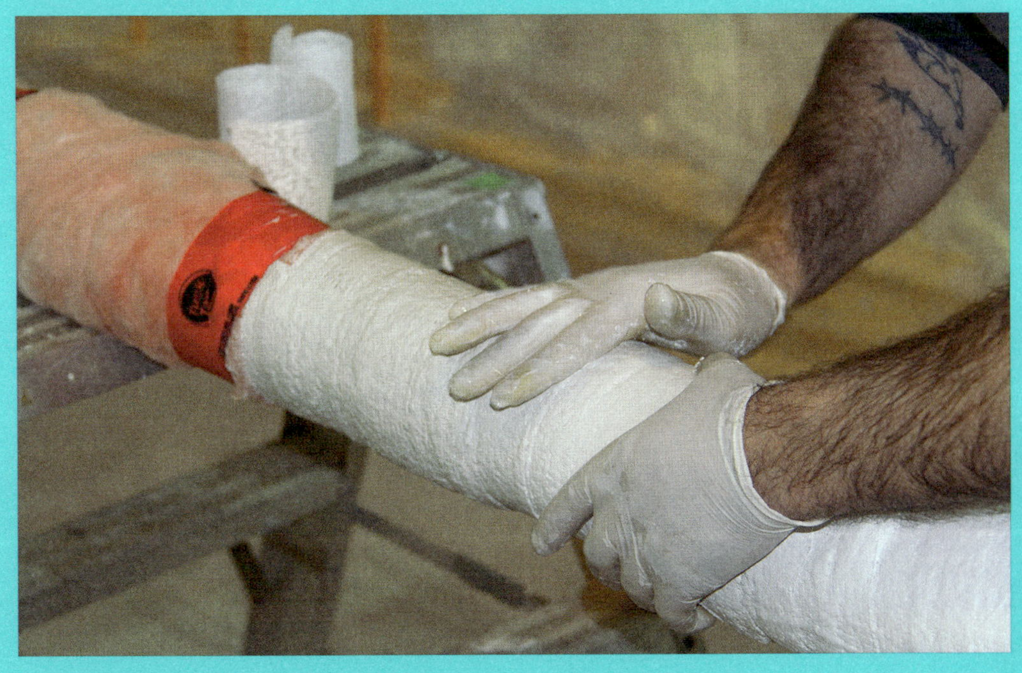

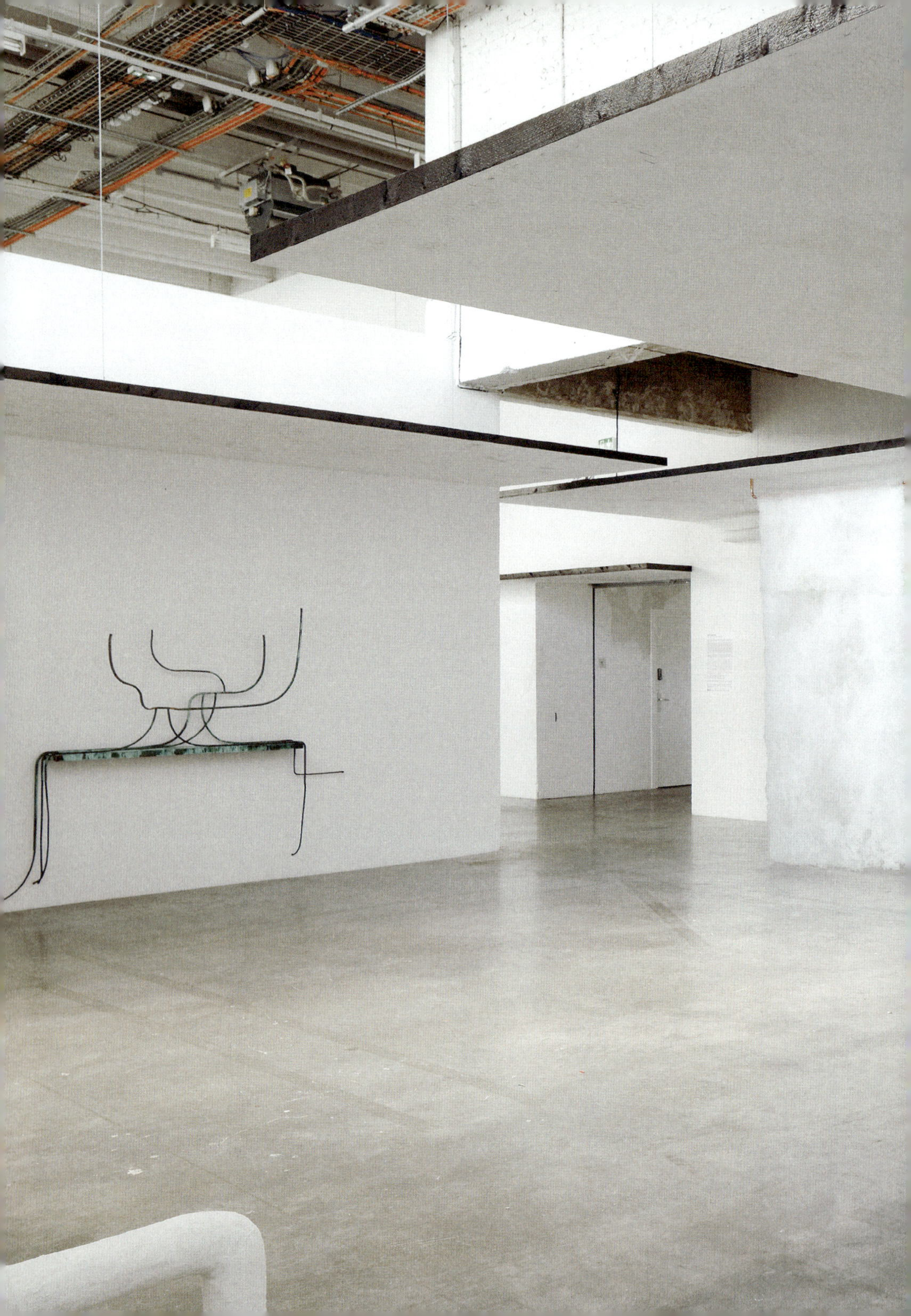

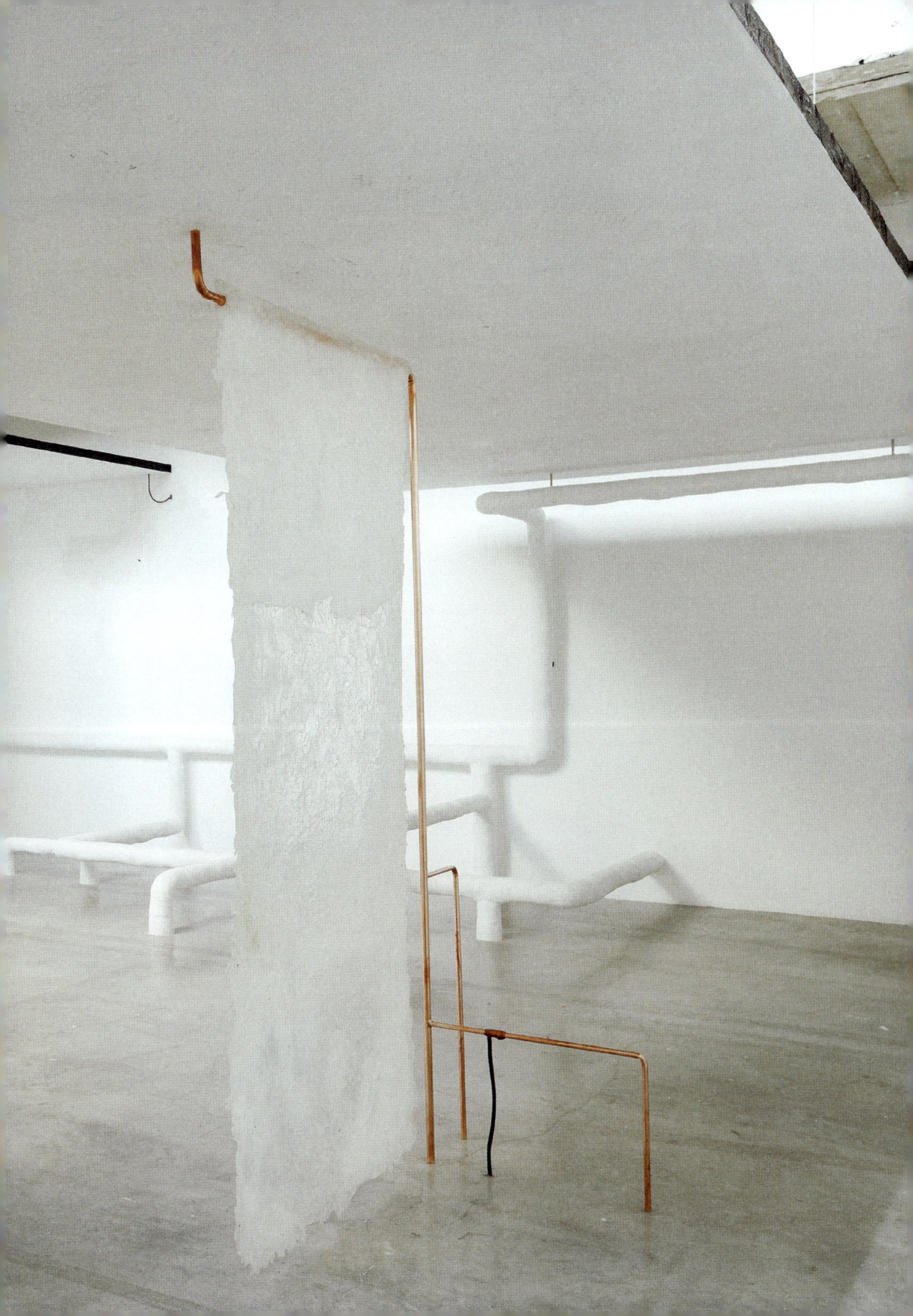

CONTRIBUTORS

WILFRID ALMENDRA, ANNE FAUCHERET, NICOLAS IDIER, ALEXANDRA MCINTOSH, NICOLAUS SCHAFHAUSEN, JORGE ARMANDO SOUSA

Wilfrid Almendra   is a French-Portuguese artist who lives and works in Marseille. His work draws upon architectural influences found in the shapes and surfaces around us. Almendra brings together diverse sources and materials to create sculptures that reference the practices of hobbyists, cite the designs of major architects of the modern era, and question social class divisions, labour, and alternative economies. Recent solo exhibitions include Clark House, Bombay (2018); Centre Bastille, Grenoble (2018); Palais de Tokyo, Paris (2017); Fogo Island Gallery, Newfoundland (2016); Les Églises, Chelles (2014); Centre d'art Passerelle, Brest; Fondation d'Entreprise Ricard (2014) and Parc Saint Léger, Paris (2013). In addition, his work has been included in numerous international exhibitions including *Singing Stones*, DuSable Museum of African American History, Chicago (2017); *Souvenirs de la vie sur terre au début du XXIème siècle*, Galerie Audi talents, Paris (2016); *The Other Sight*, CAC Vilnius (2015); *Let's Play*, Les Ateliers de Rennes (2014); *The Brancusi Effect*, Kunsthalle Wien (2014); *Parapanorama*, Palais de Tokyo, Paris (2014); *Vue d'en haut*, Centre Pompidou, Metz (2013); *Skyscraper: Art and Architecture Against Gravity*, Museum of Contemporary Art, Chicago; *Fieldwork*, Marfa (2011–12); *Prestige: Phantasmagoria of our Times*, Klaipėda Cultural Communication Center (2012); *Making Is Thinking*, Witte de With, Rotterdam (2011); *Perpetual Battles*, Baibakov Art Projects, Moscow; and *Retour vers le futur*, CAPC Bordeaux (2010), among others. Almendra was an artist-in-residence with Fogo Island Arts in 2015/16.

Anne Faucheret   is an art historian and critic. Since 2014, she has been a curator at Kunsthalle Wien, where she curated *This Is Ornamental* (2018), a solo exhibition of work by Saâdane Afif; *Work it, feel it!* (2017), examining the disciplinary mechanisms shaping contemporary bodies at work; and *The Promise of Total Automation* (2016), on the shaping of new imaginaries and subjectivities through technology, among others. In 2016 she cocurated *L'Exposition Imaginaire*, a discursive and performative project exploring the implications of digitalization on the reception of art and its musealization. She also cocurated *Present Future* at Artissima, Turin. From 2013 to 2016, she was a member of *No Future Complex*, a group of artists, curators, and thinkers experimenting with ways to articulate theory and political engagement through artistic methodologies. From 2010 to 2015, she was a curatorial advisor at the steirischer herbst festival, Graz, where she organized exhibitions including *Liquid Assets* (2013) and *Adaptation* (2012), and cocurated the 24/7 marathon-camp *Truth Is Concrete* (2012). Faucheret contributes regularly to international art magazines and publications, and co-edited the books *Truth is Concrete: A Handbook for Artistic Strategies in Real Politics* (2014) and *The Promise of Total Automation* (2016).

Nicolas Idier   is a French-language writer of European origins. Having lived in China and India for nearly a decade, he is currently based in the countryside of southwest France. Idier holds a doctorate in Chinese art from Université Paris-Sorbonne, and has authored fiction and nonfiction books haunted by a simple question: How does one stay free in a world-sized prison? As a scholar, numerous of his academic essays on China have been published including "Chinese and Indian Modernity Towards the Past: A Paradoxical Appropriation" in *Exploring Indian Modernities: Ideas and Practices* (Springer, 2018), and is a frequent speaker on the country, such as his 2018 lecture about Kang Youwei at the Collège de France, Paris. His three most recent novels have been shortlisted for major literary awards such as the Prix Décembre, the Prix Médicis, the Prix Jean Freustié de l'Académie française, the Prix Saint-Malo/Étonnants Voyageurs, and the Prix Le Figaro. The English translation of his novel *Electric Nights* (originally published by Gallimard as *Nouvelle Jeunesse*) is forthcoming in 2019 from the Delhi-based publishing house Yatra Books. Idier is currently working on an essay and a novel set in contemporary India, and is collaborating with several artists and intellectuals including Wilfrid Almendra, Makenzy Orcel, and Arundhati Roy.

Alexandra McIntosh is Director of Programs and Exhibitions at Fogo Island Arts. In collaboration with Nicolaus Schafhausen, she oversees FIA's international artist residencies, exhibitions, publications, and events, as well as the development of strategic programs and partnerships. Her projects with FIA include establishing an annual series of socially and politically engaged films and a residency dedicated to arts writing, as well as commissions and solo exhibitions with artists Wilfrid Almendra, Marlene Creates, Shezad Dawood, Ieva Epnere, Jumana Manna, Edgar Leciejewski, Isa Melsheimer, Leander Schönweger, and Augustas Serapinas. Prior to joining FIA in 2015, McIntosh was a curator at the Illingworth Kerr Gallery, Calgary, and Program Manager, Visual Arts at the Banff Centre for Arts and Creativity. Originally from Montréal, she was Coordinator of Special Projects and Cultural Affairs at Concordia University, as well as writer/editor, and later editor of CCA Online at the Canadian Centre for Architecture (CCA). She holds a BFA in Studio Arts and Art History from Concordia University and a Masters in the History and Theory of Architecture from McGill University, Montréal. She is also a member of the artist collective Centre de recherche urbaine de Montréal (CRUM).

Nicolaus Schafhausen is an internationally renowned curator based in Berlin. Director of Kunsthalle Wien from 2012 to March 2019, he is currently working on *Tell me about* ~~*yesterday*~~*tomorrow*, a major exhibition and discursive program at the Munich Documentation Centre for the History of National Socialism, opening in Fall 2019. Previously, he was Director of Witte de With Center for Contemporary Art in Rotterdam, Curator at the Nordic Institute for Contemporary Art in Helsinki (NIFCA), Director of the Frankfurter Kunstverein, and Artistic Director of Künstlerhaus Stuttgart. He was also founding director of the European Kunsthalle, an initiative to establish a new art institution in Cologne, from 2005 to 2007. Schafhausen was the curator of the German Pavilion in 2007 and 2009, and of the Kosovo Pavilion in 2015 at the Venice Biennale. He was cocurator of the first Brussels Biennale in 2008; curator of the Dutch House at Expo 2010, Shanghai; cocurator of the

55th October Salon, Belgrade (2014); and cocurator of the 6th Moscow Biennale (2015). He has also curated exhibitions at the Stedelijk Museum Amsterdam; Lenbachhaus, Munich; National Museum of Art, Architecture and Design in Oslo; and the Contemporary Art Centre (CAC), Vilnius, among others. In addition to his extensive experience in leading institutions and curating exhibitions, he is the author and editor of numerous publications on contemporary art. Schafhausen is Strategic Director of Fogo Island Arts and Shorefast.

Jorge Armando Sousa is a stonemason, farmer, and poet. He is based in Fradizela, a small village in the north of Portugal.

Fogo Island Arts is a residency-based contemporary art organization that supports research and production of new work for artists, filmmakers, writers, musicians, curators, designers, and thinkers from around the world. Since 2008, FIA has brought some of the most exciting emerging and renowned artists of today to Fogo Island, Newfoundland, Canada, to take part in residencies and to present solo exhibitions at the Fogo Island Gallery. FIA also presents programs in cities across Canada and abroad, including the Fogo Island Dialogues interdisciplinary conversation series, as part of its international outreach. Combining contemporary art, iconic architecture, and social innovation in a singular setting, FIA is a world-class institution that is uniquely rooted in community. FIA is an initiative of Shorefast, a registered Canadian charity with the mission to build economic and cultural resilience on Fogo Island.

Fogo Island Arts graciously acknowledges its Patrons, including members of the Founders' Circle, FIA Partners, and FIA Friends for their essential support of residencies, programs, and exhibitions.

POEMS

JORGE ARMANDO SOUSA

Areia água e cimento
Uma mistura potente
Usada na construção
Com betoneira a trabalhar
Carreta para a massa transportar
Colher sempre na mão
Para blocos assentar

———————————————

Sand, water, and cement
A potent blend
Used in construction
The concrete mixer revolves
A wheelbarrow carries the blend
Trowel in hand
To the bricks land

Com espírito obsoleto
As casas em esqueleto
Mostram a imagem
D´um povo, embora nobre
Ainda bastante pobre
Que labuta com coragem

———————————

With the spirit obsolete
The houses in skeletons
Depict an image
Of a people, though good
Still very poor
Toiling with courage

É no ciclo das coisas
Que até parece de doidas
Se dá a transformação
E num louco intento
As marcas do tempo
Já mais se apagarão

———————————

It's in the cycle of things
It seems an invention by the mad
That the transformation will happen
And with a mad intent
The marks of time
Will never descend

Quando o vidro fica baço
É sempre um embaraço
Na frente e ao revés
E que de repente
Deixa de ser transparente
E não se vê através

____

When glass becomes matte
It's always sad
In the front and in the back
And suddenly
It loses the transparency
And the translucency

Construídas pra habitar
Ficaram por terminar
Essas casas de betão
Em tons muito garridos
De blocos coloridos
Nelas abundam vegetação

————————————

Built to be inhabited
They were never complete
Those houses in concrete
In the midst of the vibrant tones
And colourful bricks
The vegetation pricks

De um modo em geral
Este gesto paradoxal
Até da vontade de rir
Casas não habitadas
Em condições apropriadas
Construídas pra destruir

———————————

Generally speaking
This paradoxical gesture
It's a comical treasure
Vacant houses
In appropriate conditions and polished
Constructed for being demolished

Uma planta formosa
Essa é a mimosa
Árvore de medio porte
Suas flores amarelas
E o cheiro que emana delas
Fazem nos recordar o norte
Com toda a certeza
É delirante
Que num instante
Perde a beleza

———————————————

A gorgeous plant
The mimosa
A medium-sized tree
Its yellow flowers
And its fragrance
Remind us of the north
It's maddening
The certainty
That in an instant
It loses all its beauty

Ao longo das estradas
Jamais terminadas
Casas como castelos
E nos recantos mais belos
O bruto do betão
Contrasta com o cinza
Nos jardins trabalhados
Alguns arbustos plantados
Mostrão formas como ginjas.

————————————

Alongside the roadways
Never finished
Houses like castles
In the midst of the most charming nooks and crannies
The crudeness of the concrete
Contrasts with the grey ashes
In the garden
Some planted bushes
Exhibit their morello cherry forms

Entulho a céu aberto
Eu vi aqui bem de perto
Carcaças de frigorifico
Com plásticos a mistura
Lixo de cor diferente
Que infesta o ambiente
Composto que muito dura.

———————————————

Rubble in the open air
I saw from a short distance
Fridge shells
Among plastic bags
Rubbish of different colours
Infesting the environment
Everlasting compost

COLOPHON

Wilfrid Almendra—Light Boiled Like Liquid Soap

This catalogue is published on the occasion of the exhibition *Wilfrid Almendra—Light Boiled Like Liquid Soap*, Fogo Island Gallery, March 25 to October 9, 2016.

Copublished by Fogo Island Arts and Sternberg Press

Editors: Alexandra McIntosh and Nicolaus Schafhausen
Translation: Melissa Bull (Idier), John Doherty (Faucheret, Conversation)
Copyediting and proofreading: Shanti Maharaj
Graphic design: Surface, Frankfurt am Main/Berlin, Markus Weisbeck, Lukas Wagner
Printing and binding: NINO Druck GmbH, Neustadt/Wstr.

ISBN 978-3-95679-474-2

Photo credits:
© Courtesy of the artist: 88–89
© Alexander Ferko (Courtesy of Fogo Island Arts): 4–5, 36–47, 64–71, 100–1, 116
© Aurélien Mole (Courtesy of Palais de Tokyo): 1, 90–91

Acknowledgements:

Wilfrid Almendra would like to thank Sandra Adam-Couralet, Kingman Brewster, Bénédicte Chevallier, Zita Cobb, Caroline Cournede, Aurelia Defrance, Alex Ferko, Marc Fiset, Jean de Loisy, Heather Morton, Don Paul, Nicolaus Schafhausen, and Iris Stünzi; with special thanks to Maxime Davy, Anne Faucheret, Nicolas Idier, Céline Kopp, Alexandra McIntosh, and Jorge Armando Sousa.

Fogo Island Arts
Highway 334 – Suite 100
Fogo Island, NL A0G 2X0
www.fogoislandarts.ca

Sternberg Press
Caroline Schneider
Karl-Marx-Allee 78
D-10243 Berlin
www.sternberg-press.com

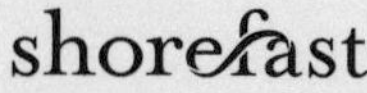
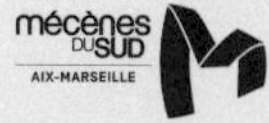

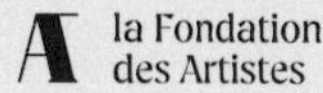

FOGO ISLAND ARTS

49° 37′ N, 54° 12′ W

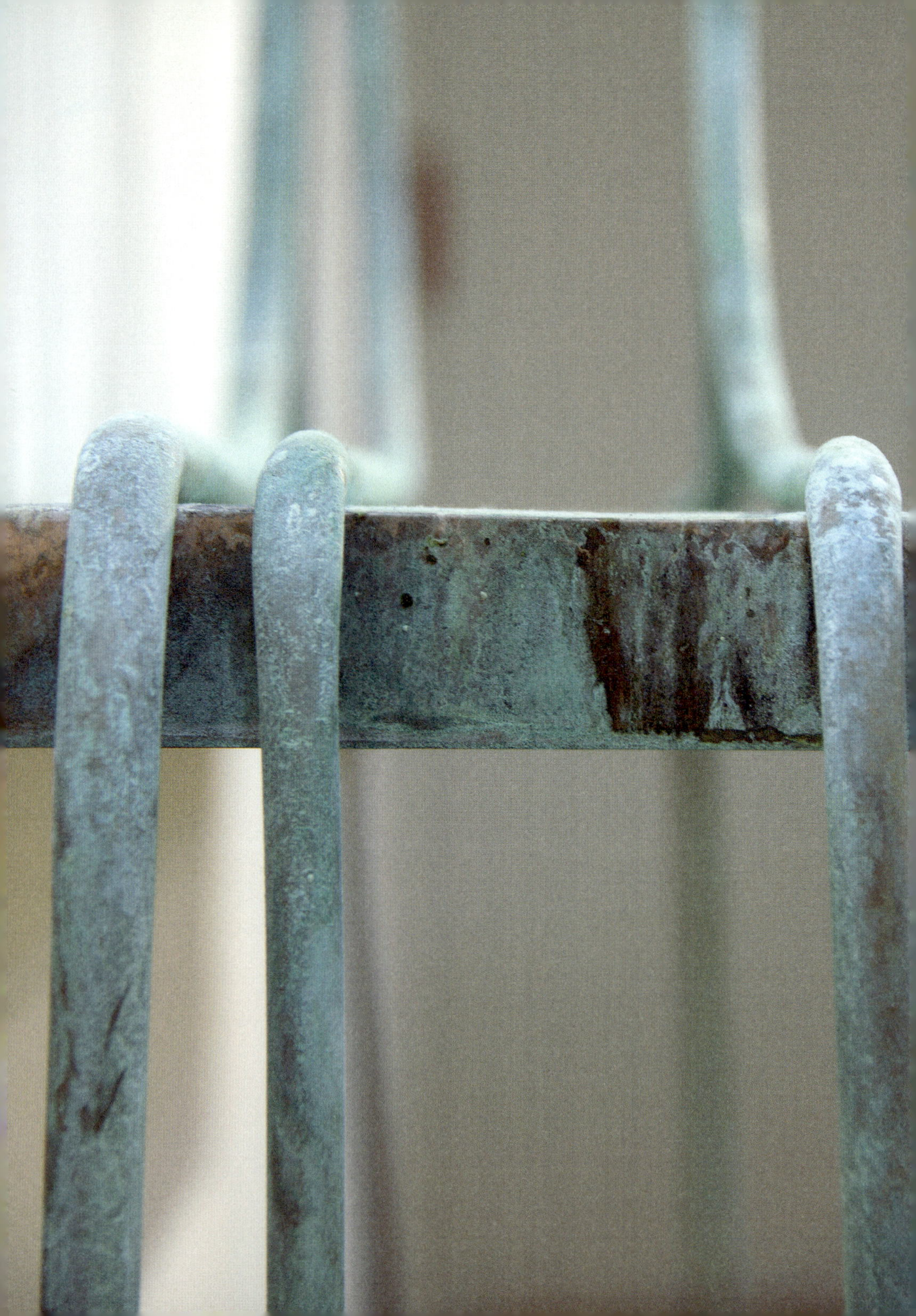